PROCLAIM!
SHARING WORDS, LIVING EXAMPLES, CHANGING LIVES

Marcus George Halley

CHURCH
PUBLISHING
INCORPORATED

Church Publishing
19 East 34th Street
New York, NY 10016
www.churchpublishing.org

Cover design by Paul Soupiset
Typeset by Rose Design

A record of this book is available from the Library of Congress.

ISBN-13: 978-1-64065-242-2 (paperback)
ISBN-13: 978-1-64065-243-9 (ebook)

CONTENTS

INTRODUCTION

I GREW UP IN CHURCH.

My fondest childhood memories are associated with church if for no other reason than that church occupied such a prominent place in my life that most of my childhood memories, good or bad, bear some association. Not only were Sundays strictly for church (and I mean *all day*—two services in the morning with Sunday school in between, followed by lunch at church, and often some other service at a neighboring congregation in the evening), but church also seeped into the other days as well. Wednesdays were for Bible study, Saturdays were for intercessory prayer and probably choir rehearsal. By the time I reached young adulthood, I was thoroughly churched but spiritually starving.

Some of my worst childhood memories are also connected to church. In many ways, it feels like I crawled into my adulthood, desperately seeking the spiritual nourishment that I had been denied as I came into the awareness of my sexuality. For reasons that continue to elude me, there are those who think God so fragile or grace so miniscule and scarce that it is their job to hoard it and protect it rather than lavish it upon all they meet. I knew I wasn't welcomed in the church of my childhood, but even though I left, the rhythm of Sunday-keeping was so strong, so naturally engrained in the rhythm of my life that I kept going to church. For years I visited church after church, never really finding a place to land for long.

All of that began to change the moment I walked into an Episcopal church in Charlotte, North Carolina. For this Southern-raised National Baptist, the words of the liturgy were expansive and pointed to a whole new world, one where mere mortals dared to approach the mystery of God holding confidence and humility, where the full witness of Holy Scripture was heard, where we embraced a connection to an ancient church that was charging headlong into the uncertain future, where simple creatures of bread and wine were deemed worthy enough to bear the actual presence of an infinite God. That first experience at the Eucharist broke my world open in ways I am still working through.

As I sit down to write this book, I am a decade into my journey with God through the Episcopal Church. I've worshiped with and served the church in the South, Midwest, and Northeast. I've raised my hands in a charismatic atmosphere, genuflected during a service of Eucharistic Adoration, sung Taize hymns around a campfire, and everything in between the matrix of wonder, love, and praise. After years of ministry and worship in the Episcopal Church, ministry that involves teaching and preaching, creating and presiding over communal worship, writing and thinking deeply about the intersection of evangelism and mission, I have come to see that what initially drew me to the worship of the Episcopal Church was something more than expansive words and beautiful ritual. What I hungered for then, and hunger for now, is an engagement with the Risen Christ that is more than an isolated moment of personal piety. I yearn for an experience of Christ that has the capacity to change me and to change the world. I want an encounter with Christ that actively participates in the continued work of Christ in the world—reconciliation, peacemaking, justice, and mercy—as we await the fullness of God's reign on earth. True, authentic Christian worship is more than a refuge from the woes of the world. It is an active engagement in the new-making of the world. It is an episode of the crashing-in of God's reign of love, a community called together by God's grace despite the tilt toward estrangement and division that plagues our broader world. It is a moment where the Church can name and claim that the Christ that has come to us, and who promises to come to us again, continues to come to us in Word and sacrament.

As a practitioner of liturgy, I have also seen that we cannot take certain assumptions for granted anymore. In a culture that transmits less and less memory of Christian practice from one generation to another, and with that practice coming under understandable scrutiny for the ways in which it has either ignored (or in some cases perpetuated) oppression and injustice, we must reclaim the importance of public liturgy as our collective worship of God that participates in the mission of God by inviting us to share in dynamic love that exists within God. For too many, the liturgy has become a hermetically sealed moment of personal piety, a one-hour experience on Sunday morning that has little to nothing to do with living into the kind of movement Jesus started. It has become too small to have anything of value to proclaim to a world in desperate need of God's saving presence.

In my view, the work that Episcopal Church has engaged under the leadership of the presiding bishop, the Most Rev. Michael Curry, has been to reclaim the value of proclamation. Our challenge in this moment seems to be responding to an initiation to go deeper in every way—deeper in discipleship, deeper in love, deeper in relationship with others. Tools like "The Way of Love" offer individuals and faith communities the tools necessary to plumb the depths of our baptismal vocation to follow Christ by inviting us to live a life that is shaped by practices such as turning toward Christ, learning about the life and way of Jesus, engaging in public worship and private prayer, and other practices. Presiding Bishop Curry has said that these practices can "train up the spirit to follow in the way of Jesus and to look something like Jesus" (Way of Love Video, Youtube). This invitation to Christian discipleship invites us to do more than simply show up on Sundays and give money. This is an invitation to believe that if this Jesus stuff matters at all, we have to get serious about practicing it. If we desire a fuller experience of the reign of God, we must enact it in our lives: we have to go across boundaries to build relationships with people who experience life differently than we do; we must seek to be a blessing to all those with whom we come into contact; and (lest we forget) we must take rest as a spiritual practice seriously.

Proclaim! is about taking this work seriously. Specifically, this is a book that holds the belief that our liturgy—our collective and public worship of God that participates in the mission of God by inviting us to share in dynamic love that exists within God—is intended to so thoroughly saturate us in God's grace that we radiate grace and love in the world. Public worship is itself an engagement with God's mission and propels us into the world empowered by the Holy Spirit to *continue* our engagement with God's mission. The coming together of the community of the faithful around Word and sacrament sits at the inflection point between being gathered and being sent. Something happens when we come close to God. Like Moses, like Mary Magdalene, like Paul, coming close to God has consequences and the invitation we are offered in public worship is to not leave the same way we came. Being gathered and being sent are two sides of the same coin of God's mission of reconciliation.

It is called *Proclaim!* for two reasons. First, the fact that we gather at all, especially on a Sunday, makes a public statement about what we believe and how we view the world—through the lens of our Lord's resurrection. Regardless of how others see the world, disciples of Jesus Christ are invited to see the world through the ongoing reality of God's new-making. Second, how we worship makes a proclamation about who we are, whose we are, and how we are to live in the world. The patterns, the rites (words), and rituals (actions) teach us to ask a different set of questions than we might otherwise ask and to make a new set of connections between God's ongoing work and our daily lives, thereby strengthening our ability to bear witness to the resurrection of Jesus Christ as apostles sent by God into the ordinariness of our world.

As a leader in a faith community, I am aware of the incredible paradigm shift this book will be for many. The shift from faith as a set of ideas privately held by individuals who perform their personal piety before the God of their own understanding back to the idea of faith as an ongoing life lived before God within which the regular gathering of an individual with the collective community of faith is an essential component to engaging in God's mission is immense. I happen to also believe that it is key to participating in God's mission. As Bishop Ian Douglas, Bishop Diocesan of the Episcopal Church in Connecticut, says repeatedly, "God has always had the Church God needs to be about the mission of God. The question is, will we be that Church?" To be *that* Church, I believe it is important to reclaim public liturgy as something more than a collection of individual relationships with God. Public liturgy must say something about God, not only to those in the room, but to those *not* in the room. It must speak the truth of God's reconciling love and break through the din of apathy, the cacophony of prejudice and oppression, and dreadful chords of isolation and alienation that threaten to break apart the fragile bonds of humanity.

The purpose of this book is to help make disciples out of people for whom public worship is either rote and unremarkable or tedious and inconvenient. This book draws connections between the practices of public worship and aspects of our ordinary lives in order to help us engage in public worship and private prayer with more attention and intention. The Bible suggests that we live in a paradox, that the kingdom of God has both come near to us and is easy to miss as we walk past it unaware. My hope is that this book will help us pay attention to the ways the kingdom of God comes close to us in public worship and shows us how to recognize the signs of it elsewhere, thereby making us participants in God's reconciling work. To do this, I've arranged this book to first explore what I mean by "God's mission" and then to explore the various ways the individual parts of the service of Holy Eucharist, the primary service of public worship for many Episcopalians, breaks open a new facet of God's mission.

My understanding of worship is shaped by regular practice of the Holy Eucharist as outlined in the Episcopal Book of Common Prayer. If you are familiar with the pattern of the Eucharist, this book will feel familiar to you because it uses that shape in order to provide a new interpretive lens through which we might see the liturgy differently. If you are unfamiliar with this pattern, this book might serve as a roadmap for that experience as well as an invitation to navigate the pattern in person in community. Regardless of whether you share the Eucharist weekly, monthly, or at some other interval, Christians across denominations gather, listen, respond, remember, share, and go. The idea behind that pattern is to not only serve as a formation tool for those interested in deepening their understanding of the Eucharist, but also to highlight the eucharistic shape of our lives—the ordinary and often unremarkable ways we gather, listen and respond, give of ourselves, and ultimately share grace with one another in ways that destroy injustice and invite us to experience episodes of God's reign. Even if you do not regularly share in the Holy Eucharist, you can benefit from understanding how the rituals and rites associated with this liturgy illuminate practices of peacemaking, community-building, and justice-seeking in our lives.

This book is for people who are deeply interested in revival—personally and in their faith communities. It is for practitioners, planners, and students of liturgy. It is for spiritual seekers, those who, like myself, found the Episcopal Church after a period of wandering and who want to go deeper. It is for those who are interested in the work of peacemaking and justice in the world and who are unsure about the intersection between the work that is the passion of their heart and their relationship with God, who is the lover of their soul. It is for those who want to engage in the spiritual practice of evangelism, but aren't sure they have the tools, knowledge, or awareness to engage that work meaningfully. My hope is that this book will invite you to consider deeply where you see connections between our worship and the world, to discern what this connection asks of you, and then to make choices that propel you in the direction of God, who is already out there in the world making all things new.

I am grateful for the work of Ruth Meyers, particularly her book *Missional Worship Worshipful Mission*, which has been an amazing guide through my thoughts. Having met Dr. Meyers a few years ago at a conference on prayer book revision in Sewanee, Tennessee, I was heartened by her encouragement to continue thinking deeply about this intersection and what resources a renewed life of the Spirit might offer me. In addition to the Bible and the Book of Common Prayer, her book, which follows the pattern of the Eucharist, along with Derek Olsen's *Inwardly Digest*, serve as the theological grounding for this book. I encourage you to read both of them as well.

I remember that day all those years ago when I took my first steps into an Episcopal Church. I could never have guessed in that moment, but that day was the beginning of a new phase of my journey with God, one that has continued to change and shape me for the work to which God has invited me. Change is hard, and formation is oftentimes painful, but the result is a life that is more attuned to purpose and mission, one shaped around the reality of the cross, and one that sounds like the gospel.

This stuff works.

The Christian life can be more than mere words and ritual. It can and, in my opinion, should be about being found by the love of God and then choosing to respond to that love by growing up into it, into what Paul the Apostle calls "the full stature of Christ" (Eph. 4:13). Liturgy opens us up to the "breathless beauty" of the "singing of angels," an experience that Howard Thurman suggests places a crown over our heads that we will spend the rest of our lives trying to grow tall enough to wear (Howard Thurman, *Deep Is the Hunger*). Changed lives cannot help but proclaim the Good News of God in Christ—in word *and* deed.

CHAPTER ONE

The Mission of God

When he came to Nazareth, where he had been brought up, he
went to the synagogue on the sabbath day, as was his custom.
He stood up to read, and the scroll of the prophet Isaiah was
given to him. He unrolled the scroll and found the place where
it was written:

> "The Spirit of the Lord is upon me,
>   because he has anointed me
>   to bring good news to the poor.
> He has sent me to proclaim release to the captives
>   and recovery of sight to the blind,
>   to let the oppressed go free,
> to proclaim the year of the Lord's favor."

And he rolled up the scroll, gave it back to the attendant, and sat
down. The eyes of all in the synagogue were fixed on him. Then
he began to say to them, "Today this scripture has been fulfilled
in your hearing."

(Luke 4:16–21)

I WAS BARELY A YEAR INTO PARISH MINISTRY when Michael Brown
was shot in Ferguson, Missouri.

Having served in racially and ideologically diverse contexts since I
was ordained a priest, I have found that this one issue is seen from a multitude of vantage points and that the mere mention of it is enough for
some people to shut down. That reality grieves me deeply. I also know
that as someone who has lived thirty-three years as an African American
in this country, this incident sparked something in me. The images of
his lifeless body lying in the street and the way law enforcement officers
were deployed to subdue the pain and anger of the Ferguson community triggered memories that I didn't even know I had. It is as if, almost
by default, this country regularly reminds black people of our place here.
The message seems to be: we can occupy public space, but not too much.

I was serving in a historically white congregation at this point. To be clear, this community admitted that they wanted to be a more ethnically and racially diverse community, but like many historically white mainline congregations, the conversation was as far as many were willing to go. In this context, I found myself needing a place of refuge and escape, a place to soothe the open wound that had been inflicted by a society that treats black lives with open contempt or subtle disregard. I found the community I needed by attending a mass meeting at a local church in Kansas City, Missouri. The meeting was billed as an opportunity to gather as a community, to grieve, and to organize. The church was located in the historically black side of the town, albeit in the wealthier part. Whereas I regularly had to cordon off my experience as a black person to engage in worship with the community I served, I was free to be me here. We came together. We wept. We sang familiar hymns. We held hands. We hugged. We prayed.

My God, we prayed.

I am too young to know what a mass meeting during the civil rights movement might have looked like, but many in that room were there when Kansas City burned. It had only been a few decades since Kansas City police officers, trying to subdue another instance of civil disturbance, threw tear gas into a youth dance in a church basement, setting off the Kansas City Riot of 1968, eventually resulting in the death of six, injuries to dozens of others, millions of dollars in property damage, and a city traumatized by division. What felt true for me in that church is that faith has been a cornerstone of the way black people in the community have not only found solace in the face of terror and oppression, but also resolve.

Several decades removed from the event, I remember most vividly the direct connection between prayer and witness. Unlike many of the church services I've experienced, the prayer of that assembly had a trajectory. It is one thing to understand the Holy Spirit as the animating force underneath and within our prayer. It is something altogether different to understand ourselves as having been taken into that force and carried into a new, inspiring reality—the kingdom of God. Prayer and worship painted a compelling vision that left the congregation yearning for a better, more just, more compassionate world.

We sang and prayed and heard scripture proclaimed and then were told how to be in the world in a way that bore witness to the inbreaking movement of justice that is part-and-parcel to the reign of Christ. There was energy in that room and that energy was given a direction and purpose—organize new justice-oriented communities, be a just presence in your sphere of influence, believe that a more compassionate world is possible despite the desperate tantrums of injustice *because* God has already won the ultimate victory. It might even be suggested that the prayers of the community gathered in that room were *eschatological*, that is, oriented toward the promise of God's future.

This experience was intentional. It drew a lot of energy and wisdom from the mass meetings of the civil rights movement. The spiritual and moral energy that supported the civil rights movement was cultivated in the Black Church, black Christian communities who trace their legacy back to the slave churches across the antebellum United States of America. These churches took on the task of reinterpreting Christian tradition in a way that was affirming of black people living in white supremacist power systems, redeeming and transforming a faith tradition white supremacy had distorted and twisted beyond recognition. Unlike their white, privileged counterparts, black Christians never had the ability to settle into Sunday performative religion because their lives were at constant risk. Part of African American Christian public worship makes clear that God is present with us and that because of God's presence, our lives are being changed and the oppressive regimes that surround us are being dismantled as God's "Great Day" comes ever more clearly into view.

The spiritual force underneath the civil rights movement was deeply rooted in scripture, such as Isaiah's prophetic vision of the "peaceable kingdom." Civil rights activists were not involved in any ordinary task. They knew themselves to be involved in work of divine importance. Churches not only supplied the space for these mass meetings to take place, they also set the tone. Nowhere is this more evident than in Martin Luther King's final speech at Mason Temple Church of God in Christ in Memphis, Tennessee, where he, invoking Moses on Mount Nebo, exclaimed:

I don't know what will happen now. We've got some difficult days ahead. But it really doesn't matter with me now, because I've been to the mountaintop. And I don't mind. Like anybody, I would like to live a long life. Longevity has its place. But I'm not concerned about that now. I just want to do God's will. And He's allowed me to go up to the mountain. And I've looked over. And I've seen the Promised Land. I may not get there with you. But I want you to know tonight, that we, as a people, will get to the promised land. And I'm happy, tonight. I'm not worried about anything. I'm not fearing any man. Mine eyes have seen the glory of the coming of the Lord. (*https://kinginstitute.stanford.edu/king-papers/documents/ive-been-mountaintop-address-delivered-bishop-charles-mason-temple*)

The context is very different and it can be argued that the privilege of white mainline denominations strips them of any urgency, but I often wonder if contemporary mainline churches have this degree of spiritual integrity and power or clarity of purpose. My sense is that we do not. Church for many is their last refuge of safety and sanity in a world gone mad, so any bandwidth for change, even personal change, has been squeezed out. The institution itself is facing such an existential crisis that energy is being diverted away from conversations about the purpose of Church and how we must deepen our call to Christian discipleship and is instead being poured into conversations about self-preservation. In this context, the function of worship then is to comfort us in what we feel is our affliction and to promise us the maximum amount of benefit with the least amount of effort. As much as we might like this to be true, this simply doesn't reflect God's mission expressed in the ministry of Jesus Christ. Jesus tells followers like us over and over again that those who seek life, abundant life, must surrender the life they have now. "If any want to become my followers, let them deny themselves and take up their cross daily and follow me" (Luke 9:23).

That call to follow is the basis of our participation in God's mission. While the attribution is misplaced and reflects the Episcopal Church's self-understanding in a particular moment, the answer to the question of mission in the prayer book is spot on. The mission of God (the Book of

Common Prayer says "mission of the Church") "is to restore all people to unity with God and each other in Christ" (Book of Common Prayer, 855). The primary actor in that mission is God, who is already out ahead of the church engaging in this transforming and liberating work. The invitation from God is to participate in this work, to join the movement as it were, to bear witness to God's kingdom. God has already said "yes" to us by securing our freedom from sin and death. No matter how worthless or unworthy we think ourselves to be, God sees such immeasurable value and worth in us that God was willing to give of God's own self to save us. To follow God therefore is to respond to God's "yes" with a "yes" of our own. Far from being a celestial fire-insurance policy, joining this movement is what it means to be a Christian.

When Jesus stands up in the synagogue to read the words of Isaiah, he is doing a series of incredibly important actions. First, he is reminding the congregation of God's work. Second, he reinterprets the meaning of that work to meet the needs of his context. It is remarkable that in reciting the words of the prophet, Jesus engages in some interesting interpretation. According to the oracle in Isaiah 61, the prophet says that God has sent him to:

- Bring good news to the oppressed (v. 1)
- Bind up the brokenhearted (v. 1)
- Proclaim liberty to the captives (v. 1)
- Release to the prisoners (v. 1)
- Proclaim the years of the Lord's favor, and the day of vengeance for our God (v. 2)

But when Jesus references Isaiah in Luke 4, he spins it. According to Jesus, God has sent him to:

- Bring good news to the poor (v. 18)
- Proclaim release to the captives (v. 18)
- Proclaim . . . *recovery of sight to the blind* (v. 18)
- Let the oppressed go free (v. 18)
- Proclaim the years of the Lord's favor (v. 19)

So much of Jesus's other words may be attributed to translation, but it is curious that the middle proclamation, the "recovery of sight to the blind," seems to be an innovation, something that we don't find at all in Isaiah 61. It seems that Jesus is making clear that not only does he stand in continuity with the Jewish prophetic tradition, but he is remixing it. Not only has he come to set people free, to heal, and to restore, but he has come so that we might see what we otherwise could not.

To understand what this seeing might be, it is important to understand the world of Luke. For Luke, time was separated into two ages, the Age of the Flesh and the Age of the Spirit. As Luke's Gospel unfolds, it becomes clear that the Incarnation, what Fleming Rutledge refers to as "the definitive invasion" of the territory that belongs to "the occupying Enemy," has inaugurated the new age of the Spirit (Rutledge, *Advent*, 19). This is reflected in the topsy-turvy nature of society captured in Mary's song—*the Magnificat*.

> And Mary said,
> "My soul magnifies the Lord,
> and my spirit rejoices in God my Savior,
> for he has looked with favor on the lowliness of his servant.
> Surely, from now on all generations will call me blessed;
> for the Mighty One has done great things for me,
> and holy is his name.
> His mercy is for those who fear him
> from generation to generation.
> He has shown strength with his arm;
> he has scattered the proud in the thoughts of their hearts.
> He has brought down the powerful from their thrones,
> and lifted up the lowly;
> he has filled the hungry with good things,
> and sent the rich away empty.
> He has helped his servant Israel,
> in remembrance of his mercy,
> according to the promise he made to our ancestors,
> to Abraham and to his descendants for ever." (Luke 1:46–55)

Just as in Jesus's later interpretation of Isaiah 61, Mary's song makes clear that what is happening in this moment is connected to something has been happening for centuries. The overturning of society was the fulfillment of a promise "made to our ancestors, to Abraham and his descendants for ever" in the same way that Jesus was the walking fulfilment of Isaiah's oracle.

Jesus's inauguration of the new Age of the Spirit did not immediately put an end to the Age of the Flesh. Rather, the Church lives in the interval between the death of the current age and the fullness of the next. As Fleming Rutledge later says, "The church is analogous to paratroopers who secure a place behind enemy lines. We are God's commandos, guerrillas, and resistance fighters in the territory occupied by the enemy, who participate in establishing 'signs and beachheads' signifying the ultimate victory" (*Advent*, 19).

What does all this have to do with mission and seeing? The Church of God is called to be the vanguard of heaven. We are those who, by God's grace, have been given a glimpse into the ultimate reality of God's reign and are thereby called by God to establish outposts of that promised reign through good works, the development of spiritual practices, and the pursuit of justice and mercy. Christians are people who commit to living lives that, in big ways and in small, speak the joy of God's coming reign. We are also those who see the ongoing renewal and re-creation of the world even in the face of existential threats like climate change and nuclear war. Far from being an excuse to abandon the world to whatever fate may come, our collective belief that God is out ahead of us renewing the world propels us out into the world in mission convinced of God's ultimate victory and the eventual triumph of justice, compassion, and peace.

At its best, the Church can be the place where God's reign is experienced more clearly than anywhere else. As the community of disciples gathered around the Risen Christ, we affirm, simply by our gathering that the relentlessness of life, not the yawning abyss of death, has the final say. We have compassion, justice, vulnerability, bravery, joy, and peace written deep in our communal DNA, even if centuries of schism, heresy, contention, and injustice have obscured them. Whatever else we are and whatever else we do, it has been given to us to bear witness to the kingdom of God on the earth by building communities capable of bearing the light of Christ into the darkness of the world.

The worshiping community where I have most clearly seen the crashing-in of the reign of God was during my yearlong internship with Church of Common Ground. The Church of Common Ground is a ministry of the Episcopal Diocese of Atlanta that worships, builds community with, and advocates alongside members of Atlanta's homeless community. This community worships outdoors 52 Sundays a year, singing and praying under an awning or tent when the weather becomes inclement. When I was there, the church had a storefront location that housed their support ministries: a daily Bible study, support groups, numerous AA meetings, a weekly foot clinic, and a space where folks could come in, grab a drink of cool water, charge their phones, receive their mail, or clear the chairs out of the way to stretch out on the floor and take a nap. What I witnessed in this community each day was drama and chaos, but also a church that intentionally gave their prayers direction and focus. They prayed for dignity to be shown to those who experience poverty and homelessness and then invited people from so-called "big-steeple" congregations and wealthy neighborhoods to worship and build relationship and community with them. They prayed for ways to deal with hunger and then made sandwiches and incredibly strong and often bitter church coffee, offering them freely to whoever asked. They prayed for forgiveness of their sins and then opened their hands to receive the bread and wine, surrendering bits of their guilt and shame in the process, exchanging them for morsels of the bread of angels. This community showed me the degree to which it is possible for us to be radically changed in worship by paying attention to the ways that the kingdom of God comes very near to us if we are open and vulnerable enough to experience worship just beyond the edge of what makes us comfortable.

Church of the Common Ground is where worship-as-mission first came alive to me.

When I served in Missouri, I stumbled into facilitating the anti-racism trainings required for ordination. I worked with a small team of folks who would drive many miles to offer this training to those who needed it. When I first began, I expected it to be a miserable process that people had to be coerced into. From feedback forms, that is what many participants expected as well. What my team and I worked hard to do was to establish brave and courageous space where learning could happen without shame and where participants could be inspired to make changes in their faith communities that might open them up to relationships imperiled by the subtle (and not-so-subtle) white supremacy that stalks many of our faith communities.

There would always come a moment though, when, as a trainer, I could tell when I had run up against a participants' red line. No matter how much we discussed the challenges and joys of building authentic relationships across difference or how much we highlighted God's mission of reconciliation into which we have been called, there would inevitably come a point where individuals simply were unwilling to go. Maybe it was the monochromatic images in church art and architecture, monolinguistic liturgies, or monocultural expressions of worship that convey a message about who belongs in that community and, by default, who does not. There was always something that people were unwilling to hand off in order to experience the kind of fuller expression of God's kingdom we only experience when we worship with people different from us. When worship becomes an extension of our own personal piety divorced from any sense of God's mission, it becomes an idol of our own making, a carefully curated religious artifact that struggles to convey and communicate the transforming grace of God. Instead of a liturgy of the reign of God, all we are left with in that moment is a liturgy of the status quo.

When Jesus stands up in the synagogue to read from the scroll of the prophet Isaiah, he lets the community know that the status quo has come to an end, that a new day is dawning, that the very thing for which generations of God's people had prayed had finally come to pass. It is my belief that when we gather as followers of Jesus Christ, we do so in the same spirit. Whether our communities gather in storefronts, or campus chapels, or basements, or school gyms, or parks, or neogothic structures, we proclaim that a new day is dawning not just for the world at large, but for the community within which we gather.

Each time we gather, we repeat the words of John's Revelation: *See, I am making all things new.* The deepest prayers of a community—healing from trauma, freedom from addiction, reconciliation from years of structural racism, hope in the middle of economic strain, deep relationships in a culture of increasing isolation—are all caught up in the prayers and witness of the local church, *if we are paying attention and are willing to get dirty.* We declare that there is healing, there is freedom, there is reconciliation, there is hope, there is community. In *Being Christian: Baptism, Bible, Eucharist, and Prayer*, Rowan Williams raises and then answers a question about the location of a Christian community vis-à-vis suffering and chaos. He writes:

> If we ask the question, "Where might you expect to find the baptized?" one answer is, "In the neighborhood of chaos." It means you might expect to find Christian people near to those places where humanity is most at risk, where humanity is most disordered, disfigured and needy. Christians will be found in the neighborhood of Jesus—but Jesus is found in the neighborhood of human confusion and suffering, defenselessly alongside those in need. If being baptized is being led to where Jesus is, then being baptized is being led towards the chaos and the neediness of a humanity that has forgotten its own destiny. (Williams, *Being Christian*, 4–5)

The Church stands in a paradox—at the meeting and overlap of two ages—one that is passing away and another that is on the rise. We stand with Jesus and Mary, announcing the arrival of the promise of God even as we wait on its fullness. It is our work to take our place in the messiest places in our communities, where abuse and neglect erode human relationships, where addiction and violence corrode human dignity, where poverty and oppression stifle the human spirit, and to declare—by word and example—the Good News of God in Christ. Public liturgy in that context can't always be staid and safe. The joy of our prayers is mingled with the grief of human suffering, our Alleluias cohabitate with groaning and weeping.

But we stand anyway, because God's Spirit is here, and where the Spirit of the Lord is, there is liberty.

CHAPTER TWO

What Are We Doing Here?

Then the Lord said to Moses, "Pharaoh's heart is hardened; he refuses to let the people go. Go to Pharaoh in the morning, as he is going out to the water; stand by at the river bank to meet him, and take in your hand the staff that was turned into a snake. Say to him, "The Lord, the God of the Hebrews, sent me to you to say, 'Let my people go, so that they may worship me in the wilderness.'"

(Exod. 7:14–16a)

SEWANEE, TENNESSEE, HAS BEEN HOME to me ever since I first entered the "domain" as a prospective student searching for an Episcopal seminary where I could complete my Anglican year. Years later, when the then dean asked me to return to be a part of a conversation on liturgical renewal, I jumped at the opportunity. At the point, I had served two congregations—one in Kansas City, Missouri; the other in Minneapolis, Minnesota—both of whom sought to renew themselves through a deeper engagement with liturgy. Though the two congregations represent two different contexts and histories, they were united in this reality: they were hungry for renewal, but woefully unaware of what renewal would require of community.

The first congregation—a large, established, traditional congregation in an affluent neighborhood in Kansas City, Missouri—was doing "well." They had a large budget, multiple clergy and lay staff members, and an average Sunday attendance in the mid- to high two hundreds. The leadership of church had developed the foresight to see a few years down the line and recognize that unless they did something different, they were about to experience a sharp decline. I was happy to come alongside them as an associate priest, to learn from and grow with them, and together we engaged in some innovative work around the margins of the community—creating small groups for artists with a worship- and community-building component. We also experimented with raising up a seeker community defined by question-asking that led to seeking the wisdom of the broader community. The system, like all systems, struggled when it came to substantial innovation at the heart of the community.

The second congregation—a small, scrappy congregation in Minneapolis—wasn't always so small. In living memory, the pews were full and future was bright. The decline that brought the church to the place it currently found itself was swift. As the new rector of the congregation, I had conversations with many former members, and the message I got was that many of them fled the advance of liberal theology, or communal in-fighting, or had problems with my predecessor being the first female rector in the parish's history. As the first black, openly gay rector in the parish's history, I was clear many of them would not be coming back. For the ones who remained, they coalesced around the importance of liturgy in their communal life. By the time I arrived, the church was mainly a Sunday parish with little communal, missional, or liturgical life outside of Sunday mornings.

After observing for a few months, listening to where the Holy Spirit was alive in the community, I discovered that people were incredibly interested in liturgy and yet the worship life of the community felt stagnant. After a bit more inquiry, I located the problem—the community had engaged in a lot of revision around liturgy—swapping out different prayers and experimenting with different ways of using space—without deep, substantive formation in the prayer book tradition. The questions often asked by people involved with creating worship in the community were "what did you *like*" or "what didn't you *like*." It was a step of desperation, the result of an earnest desire to experience revival and renewal.

What I have learned from a few years of parish leadership is this: the revival and renewal many faith communities seek will require engaging the complex feelings that come with discomfort and dislocation. I've also learned that people seldomly volunteer to be uncomfortable. Despite the fact that discomfort is at the heart of the Christian story ("take up your *cross* and follow" sure isn't an invitation to an all-inclusive spa), Western Christianity's centuries-long alliance with power has managed to iron out our collective capacity for discomfort for the sake of God's mission. In a time when Western Christianity is being asked to summon up the skills, resources, and capacity to engage this missional age for the sake of the gospel of Jesus Christ, we are finding it hard to show up and demonstrate resilience. I wonder how much of this is enshrined in the worship life of many faith communities. If the questions about the community's worship come down to what we "like," it is clear that we aren't terribly interested in transformation and renewal. It might be that we are more interested in the status quo than we are ready to admit, at least out loud.

I took both of these experiences with me to Sewanee, Tennessee, as well as my own experience of a deepening devotional life framed by the Daily Office and other forms of Christian prayer. Though I am sure I said it clumsily, what I tried to say in Sewanee was this: *whether or not we undergo prayer book revision, what we actually need is a dedication and commitment to a vibrant spirituality expressed both in public and private prayer.* The way we worship in the Episcopal Church, with common texts that span centuries of wisdom and striving to know and be known by Christ—when expansive, transforming, and poetic—can support our journey to and with God. My own experience of coming to the prayer book tradition as one "thoroughly churched and spiritually starving" showed me that there was spiritual sustenance here, a way of life that, when engaged with intention and openness, can serve as a guide to a deep relationship with Jesus Christ. God knows it is not perfect. Nothing human is. Though much of the prayer book is lifted directly from the Bible, it is distilled through centuries of human minds grappling with the untouchable reality of God.

I wanted my congregation to experience the renewal I had experienced—a deeper commitment to Christ, a more vibrant devotional life, a deeper awareness of the hand of God at work in the world around us, and a conviction about the power behind the truth of the gospel—and I knew that the only way to do that was to pray. Often. I came to know intimately what Rabbi Edwin Friedman means when he talks about what it means for a leader to change a system. It is tempting to think that change in a system happens by the fiat of a charismatic leader, but I have found that the change in systems occurs when leaders commit to changing. When a community's leaders—lay and ordained—make up in the minds to *be* different, the community will follow suit. As members of a community, we are ultimately only capable of changing ourselves and then inviting others to be changed as a result. The revival we seek must be cultivated in ourselves before it can ever be experienced in community.

I also picked up on something else. Our participation in public worship—however constructed—is unfathomably radical. It is a protest against the prevailing powers of this age that seek to dehumanize and degrade. Worship is a resistance against narratives of inescapable divisiveness, estrangement, isolation, and secularism. When we worship, whether we know it or not, we are representing the entire Christian community gathered across the world in storefronts, cathedrals, chapels, dorm rooms, and taverns. We are also connected to Christians who have gathered across time in catacombs, houses, in the desert, and on mountaintops. Public worship is a declaration of the reality of a new world, one that is all around us and constantly adventing upon us. When we worship God as a community of believers, we affirm our belief in the freedom of that new world and our freedom from the bondage of this one.

When we hear the story of the Exodus, we often hear God telling Moses to tell Pharaoh, "Let my people go!" What we miss is the statement connected to that demand, a statement that puts that demand into context. God tells Moses to tell Pharaoh, "Let my people go, *so that they may worship me in the wilderness*" (Exod. 7:16, emphasis added). This demand is repeated several times and is met with Pharaoh's obstinate refusal to relinquish his control over the Hebrew people. At one point in the story, after the fourth plague, Pharaoh makes a bargain. He will allow the Israelites to make a sacrifice *within* the land of Egypt. Moses rejects the bargain, stating that the kind of worship that the Israelites are being asked to do would be "offensive" to Egyptians. Pharaoh comes back with another bargain: the Israelites could go outside of Egypt, but not too far. Moses seems to agree to this demand, but as soon as he leaves, Pharaoh changes his mind. He seems to know that there is something about this God of the Israelites that won't be satisfied with momentary freedom. This exchange reveals something about the nature of worshiping the God of the Exodus—whatever else God seems to be concerned about, God is concerned about freedom. Social movements through history have shown us that once you fan the flames of freedom in the hearts of the oppressed, it may dim, but it will never be extinguished. Pharaoh knew this. Dictators and tyrants throughout human history have known this. Aware that the jig was up, God's demand of Pharaoh by way of Moses changes after that exchange. "Let my people go, so that they may worship me." God didn't need to stipulate "in the wilderness" anymore because it became clear that to worship God was to leave slavery and oppression behind.

Looking back, I wonder if the transformation both churches desired—and I think might be desired across much of Western Christianity—can be found in understanding worship as the exchange of one world—one that is dying—for another—one that is being made new. The Exodus narrative teaches us that the worship of God requires a shift in location. It is difficult, impossible even, to authentically worship God while participating—even passively—in dehumanizing, oppressive, and violent systems. To worship God, we must be willing to stand outside of those systems, to see them for what they are, to see the ways they are doomed to destruction, and then, if we must reenter them, to do so with greater clarity about the ways the mission of God calls us to engage them. If this is how we understand public liturgy, then it can never simply be "the work of the people." It has to be something more or else it is powerless to stand against the otherwise overwhelming tide of slavery that mutates and manifests in every generation.

The idea of liturgy as the "work of the people" was popularized during the liturgical renewal movement of the mid-twentieth century when churches became interested in expanding the voices present within the Eucharist beyond those called to ordered ministry. The wisdom behind this move is that worship is something *we all do*. Prayer and worship aren't the sole possession of a few ordained people with the rest of us left only to passively participate as spectators. As our current prayer book rightly states, "The entire Christian assembly participates" in the worship of the Church (BCP, 13). Ruth Meyers astutely points out that although the purpose behind liturgy as "the work of the people" was to decenter liturgy as the work of the clergy of which the people are only spectators, "by not also turning our attention beyond ourselves to the need of the world for God's reconciling love, continuing to think of liturgy as 'the work of the people' impoverishes our celebrations" (*Missional Worship Worshipful Mission*, 29).

In its original Greek context, "liturgy" or *leitourgia* referred to the public work a citizen might do for the community, particularly in terms of a public works project sponsored by an affluent citizen to benefit the masses who were not as affluent. As Meyers points out, over time the word gradually assumed a more spiritual tone with it eventually coming to mean "service, whether rendered to God or to the community" (*Missional Worship*, 27). A truly Christian understanding of liturgy reaches its climax when we understand Jesus as liturgy. Jesus is God's *leitourgia* for the sake of the world. In his self-offering, he was giving something to humanity that we desperately needed but had no way of getting on our own—reconciliation. If this is true, if sending the Son of God into the world for the sake of the renewal of Creation is God's greatest "public works project," then what might it mean to understand ourselves—our worship, our prayer, or lives of discipleship—as continued participation in God's continued self-offering? What if every single time we gathered in Christian community to pray and worship, we also continued to make present the mystery of God's love for our communities, for those in need of loving community, for those in need of reconciliation, for those whose lives are in desperate need of meaning? What if we became aware of the power that animates the Christian community and the grace that compels us to bear witness, not only to the resurrection 2,000 years ago, but to the pulses of newness that emanate from the empty tomb? What if worship led us to ask one question over and over again: how is my freedom in God, given to me by God's own self-offering, inviting me to share that freedom with others by giving myself away for the sake of those I don't even know?

We'd have revival.

In response to my community's need for formation in the prayer book tradition, I invited a few members to read Derek Olsen's *Inwardly Digest*. As a runner, I appreciated Olsen's use of athletic metaphors for the discipline of prayer and worship. Like training for a 5K, developing a vibrant devotional life requires constancy and commitment, even when it becomes dull. "You can't manipulate the Spirit," Olsen writes, "and you can't manipulate long-term formation. The point of a solid devotional practice is not momentary surges of emotion; long-term formation and transformation is measured in years and decades. Sometimes good and worthwhile devotional practices will inspire us—and sometimes they may feel more like work for long stretches of time" (*Inwardly Digest*, 17). Prayer and worship are boring sometimes and yet the transformation we seek requires us to push through, to remain dedicated, to keep our eyes on the prize. Moreover, the transformation we long for in the world requires us to remain steadfast in our work, continuing to make the love of God present in the gathering together of Christian community.

One benefit to understanding worship as God's work within which we participate is the gift of the long view. We can't expect instant transformation—either personally or in our faith communities. We are participating in God's ongoing work of renewing and transforming Creation, work that has been taking place over the course of millennia. To the degree that we are transformed by the grace of God, we are microcosms of God's ongoing work. Our private prayer and public worship are not only training us for this work, *they are active and ongoing engagements with this work.*

Never has this been more evident to me than when I was living in Kansas City, Missouri, when Michael Brown was shot. In the aftermath of the shooting, I found myself struggling to understand what it meant to be black in the United States. My faith in America's ability to actually make true on its original promise of "liberty and justice for all" died next to Michael Brown, exposed for all the world to see on Florissant Avenue. My upbringing as a Baptist had taught me that my relationship with Jesus Christ was personal, that I "could go to God in prayer," that Jesus was a friend, that "earth had no sorrow that heaven could not heal." But I found my experience in a historically white congregation challenging to say the least. If the oozing wound of American white supremacy was mentioned at all, it was mentioned in overly simplistic terms. "We have to learn to forgive," one white minister said, "only then can we achieve reconciliation."

He wasn't wrong, but it was tone-deaf for sure.

While reconciliation is the goal—and God's mission—in that moment we were dealing with bodies in the street, a community in turmoil, and individuals experiencing an incredible amount of pain. Platitudes about loving your neighbor aren't helpful when our society has grossly distorted neighborliness and often frames relationships across racial or any other difference as impossible and unequal. What we need is an intervention. What we need is a new framework for law enforcement that helps them dismantle the implicit bias taught to them by the dominant narratives of a racialized society. What we need is for black people and other people of color to be able to occupy public space without fear of running into the wrong police officer who either understands their role as judge, jury, and executioner or simply is so immersed in a culture that constantly sends negative messages about black people that they respond to a black person as an automatic threat, guilty of something until posthumously proven innocent in a court of law.

In need of healing and compassionate community, I attended an event organized by local community activists in Kansas City just a few days into the firestorm that was enveloping Ferguson, Missouri. A few community organizations had joined together to organize a march and protest in Mill Creek Park, just across the street from a major shopping district in the city. The entire event was powerful as the black community and antiracist allies from across the region joined together to grieve the ongoing assault on black bodies and to find a way to organize to continue the monumental task of dismantling racism from the institutions of our communities.

I couldn't find solace in Christian community, so I found it in the street. The Holy Spirit is known to stir beyond our gates called beautiful.

I was particularly moved when an elder from the community, a black woman with her hair styled in long, salt-and-pepper locks, stood up on a platform, grabbed a megaphone, and apologized to the younger activists and participants. "We are sorry that we didn't teach you the truth about our struggle. We were afraid we would give you a too-small view of the world and we wanted you to soar. But what we did was allow you to believe that this wasn't possible, that the hatred some folks have for you—just because you breathe—died a long time ago, when it didn't. It's here and y'all are dying."

I didn't even know I needed to hear those words and yet, as I stood in the middle of that field, buzzing with activity, somber and mournful, her words washed over me like an ocean. That moment personified the old hymn:

> There is a balm in Gilead,
> to make the wounded whole.
> There is a balm in Gilead,
> to heal the sin-sick soul.

(*Lift Every Voice and Sing*, hymn 203)

I don't remember leaving that action with any plan, any organizing strategy, any idea of how were going to walk together differently as a community in the wake of the extrajudicial killings of Michael Brown, and Tamir Rice, and Sandra Bland, and Akai Gurley, and . . . and . . . and . . . , and yet I walked away holding a bit more hope than I showed up with. That a community dared to assemble to grieve together in public, to love one another publicly, and to hold each other up gave me that hope.

I also left that gathering feeling empowered. Even though I was standing in a field—an indistinguishable face in a field of hundreds—I left feeling more seen then I had felt in weeks, or months, or years. A few days later, moved to action, I picked up the phone and called a congregation in Ferguson, Missouri, and asked their priest a simple question, "What do you need?"

"We need backpacks and school supplies. When the unrest dies down, kids will need to go back to school, but parents are afraid to go out to buy supplies."

"Got it."

With just a few days to organize, I sent out a few e-mails and mobilized my congregation and a few neighboring ones to donate school supplies. The local news even ran a story on it. Parishioners and folks in the community who couldn't make it to the local stores to buy supplies came by my office with checks and cash. "Get what you need," they said. I don't remember the quantity of backpacks and school supplies I collected. I do remember that it exceeded my goal. By the time I loaded up my car to take the donated supplies across Missouri, they filled the trunk, backseat, and passenger seat. I remember feeling secure and powerful as I drove down Interstate 40 from Kansas City to Saint Louis, like in this small, simple action, I had resisted the narrative that hopelessness and powerlessness are inevitable realities in the face of white supremacy, like I get to make choices about how I exist in the world and I can choose to use power in a way that seeks the well-being of another.

And all because I felt seen.

That action in Kansas City was not only a way to train us for the work of dismantling racist, white power structures across the institutions of our communities, but it was an *active participation therein*. We gathered to learn to love each other by loving each other, to learn to stand with one another by standing together, by learning to hold each other up by holding one another up in moments of grief. This was on-the-job training, not an antiracism training in the sterile and controlled environment of a seminar room. We were live and in living color and I left empowered.

The way we worship God should not make us feel invisible and nameless, not if we believe that we worship a God who knows each of us by name and calls us "beloved." Although we are swept up into the relentless current of God's love in worship and prayer, we do so, not to escape this world with all its joys and pains, but to better understand ourselves and our place in this world. If devotion to Christ is an *active* participation in his work of reconciliation and liberation, then we should flow out of our closer encounters with Christ in the direction of freedom.

I also left wondering about the ways I might leave a gathering of Christian worship feeling this same way. We gather, we claim space as holy, we listen and respond to scripture, we tell truths about ourselves and receive God's grace for the places in our lives where we are prone to wander, we share peace, and we make Christ present in bread and wine before sharing in the banquet of the kingdom of heaven. How do we do all of this and leave lonely, bitter, unmoved, ungracious, and overwhelmed by the brokenness of our world? Is it because we think we are in a training in the controlled environment of a seminar room?

I was teaching a newcomer class once when a question about the Holy Eucharist came up. "What are we doing in the Eucharist?" someone asked. "Like, what is happening in that moment?"

"We're rehearsing for heaven!" someone blurted out.

They weren't *wrong*, but it wasn't the whole truth.

"When we share the bread and the wine, Christ is here, right now." I said. "We don't have to wait until death to share the gifts of the kingdom of God. It comes near to us when we gather, when we share, and when we go."

Our prayer and worship aren't seminars in controlled environments where we talk *about* God. When we pray, we are coming into intimate, close relationship with God through Jesus Christ. And don't let us dare to gather in community. That's where it really goes down. Jesus tells us about the power of assembling in Christian community. "Truly I tell you," he says, "if two of you agree on earth about anything you ask, it will be done for you by my Father in heaven. For where two or three are gathered in my name, I am there among them" (Matt, 18:19–20). This statement echoes an excerpt from Ecclesiastes where the teacher says, "Though one might prevail against another, two will withstand one. A threefold cord is not quickly broken" (Eccles. 4:12). There is power in numbers and something very real happens when we dare to gather in community and recognize Christ in our midst.

I long deeply for community, especially community that is bigger than itself. Understanding Christian community as subversively powerful and purposefully understated has reshaped my relationship to Christ and his Church. As we navigate the shifting tectonic plates of rapidly changing religious landscape, I have gained solace from the realization that we never need armies to accompany the gospel. We never need wealth, and power, and prestige to aid in our evangelism. All we need is a heart keenly aware that the Son of the Living God is present here, that this community gathered in humility around prayer and sacrament is the vanguard of the reign of Christ, that we are actively participating in the tearing down of oppressive power structures by affirming the sovereignty of God over every earthly power.

This message is clear in Exodus, but that message got lost somewhere in the centuries.

The moment the Roman Empire found out that there was a benefit to co-opting the community of disciples gathered around the Risen Christ, the message of movement began to become distorted. Before long, armies bore the cross of the Prince of Peace into battle, killing others in Christ's name. This only grew worse as the faith spread and more and more people in power took on the name of Jesus Christ without committing to one of the principles of his movement—love. Soon, the message of Christianity was almost indistinguishable from warfare, colonialism, and oppression. All over the world, the Cross of Christ wreaked havoc among unsuspecting peoples and cultures. Far from being a movement of perpetual liberation—a never-ending Jubilee—the community of faith around Jesus of Nazareth became a principality, a power-broker, the very thing the reign of Christ came to dethrone.

And yet—by the sheer power of the of the Holy Spirit—the message of the Crucified and Risen One still managed to be told and lived. By mystics in deserts, monastics in communities, slaves deep in the woods of the American South, the earth-shattering truth of Christ continued to be proclaimed and shared. These individuals and communities fell in love with Jesus Christ and—against all odds—preserved a faith that had been distorted beyond recognition by the allure of power and wealth.

As a young disciple of Jesus Christ—one who will likely be alive to see the Church in the West forced to reform itself—I actually believe that we are being given a gift. Our wider culture, having discovered it no longer needs us to be an avenue of power, is tossing us off to the side. We no longer have pride-of-place in the public square, Sunday's aren't just for church anymore, and most people are apathetic to the Church. All we are left with is Christ and, to borrow from C. S. Lewis, the one who has Christ and everything has no more than the one who has Christ alone (C. S. Lewis, *The Weight of Glory*, 34).

In short, we are set up for revival.

The Pentecost story tells us that in the days immediately following the crucifixion, resurrection, and ascension of Jesus, the disciples were trapped in a cyclical pattern of locking themselves in rooms. They had just experienced the greatest trauma of their lives coupled with witnessing something so wonderful, they struggled to find words to speak about it. They were afraid of sharing the news of the resurrection, afraid of openly proclaiming the gospel of Jesus Christ, and uncertain about their future. They went through the formalities of ensuring the future of the movement by electing Matthias—the Church is very good at formalities—but deep down, there was a deep, saturating fear.

And they dared to gather in the real world. They were just waiting for something to happen.

When 110 of them were altogether, the Holy Spirit came and blew them into action. Peter preached a sermon so powerful that thousands of people were brought into the body of Christ. The Church was set on a course that day that—though it may have stumbled over the centuries—it remains on to this very day. We are the Church of Jesus Christ, a mystical extension of his body in the world, called to go where he went, say what he said, and hang out with the folks he hung out with—the misfits, the outcasts, the struggling, the lost, the lonely, and the hurting. If prayer and worship bring us close to Jesus, it should bring us close to those who are suffering. If is isn't, we might be guilty of idolatry, worshiping a projection of ourselves instead of worshiping the "stone the builders rejected." My experience shows me that idolatry is seductive because fidelity to the living God actually requires something different from us than we are wont to give. That might explain why people are so apt to walk away from faith the moment they are asked to behave differently. When we're used to doing whatever we want with divine approval, being told that God might require conversion feels like death.

And that might just be the point.

Jesus tells his disciples that those who would be his disciples are to deny themselves, take up their cross, and follow him. This is nothing short of an invitation to die—die to a world that is itself dying in order that we might be born anew in a world that is coming. Personal prayer and public worship are part of that process, bringing us close to the consuming fire of God and giving God more and more of ourselves to refine and purify.

Our worship and prayer is also something else. When we pray individually or worship in the context of Christian community— whether we use a set of texts or not—we are not only swept up in God's liberating love of the world, we are swept up in God's very self. That we are referred to as the "body of Christ" throughout much of scripture is neither accidental nor inconsequential. When we pray and worship, we become aware of our connection to Jesus Christ who is at the same time "one with the Father."

When Jesus's disciples came to him, seeking wisdom on how to pray, Jesus tells them, "When you pray, say 'Our Father . . .'" At face value, referring to God as "Father" represents a particular ancient worldview where men were seen as the "fountain of life," which has since been debunked by modern science. Setting aside for the moment the patriarchal effects of the word, the analogy is meant to draw a distinction between "Creator," which assumes that what is created is fundamentally separate and disconnected from the creator, and "Father," which assumes that what is begotten is fundamentally connected to the parent, even if that begetting is through adoption.

The analogy goes deeper than this, though. By inviting his disciples to refer to God as "Father," Jesus is inviting them into a deeper, more profound, more intimate relationship than simply "Creator." Jesus didn't come merely to make us *better*. Jesus came to make us *new*. In *Mere Christianity*, C. S. Lewis writes that,

> a world of nice people, convinced of their own niceness, looking no farther, turned away from God, would be just as desperately in need of salvation as a miserable world—and might even be more difficult to save. For mere improvement is not redemption . . . God became man to turn creatures into sons: not simply to produce better men of the old kind but to produce a new kind of man. (Lewis, *Mere Christianity*, in *The Completely C. S. Lewis Signature Classics*, 170)

Understanding Lewis's use of "sons" and "men" as patriarchal language that reflects his time, words that within his context would have been understood to be inclusive of all people, his thought here is powerful. Jesus invites us into intimate relationship with him so that we can share his intimate relationship with his Source, the "Fountain of Life" from whom all things come. As the prayer book outlines, prayer is simply "response to God" whereas Christian prayer is "response to God the Father, through Jesus Christ, in the power of the Holy Spirit" (BCP, 856). The distinction is key. To pray—publicly or privately— is to take on a new identity, to walk in a new world, and to affirm a whole new set of allegiances and perspectives.

At its heart, our desire to pray to God in private or worship God in the context of Christian community is Jesus's very desire to commune with the Father. To pray as a Christian is "to let Jesus' prayer happen" in us (Williams, *Being Christian*, 62). It is finally saying "yes" to the desire that is present in each of us that otherwise manifests in workaholism, greed and acquisitiveness, and busyness, namely, the desire to fill the God-sized hole in each of us, the parts of ourselves that need that which is beyond us to give us meaning.

We might like to think that it is something more than this, but our worship—whether set rites and rituals or not—is to God as a boat is to a raging sea. It is the only thing keeping us afloat in the middle of what would otherwise overwhelm us and yet, as scripture narrates for us in the story of Peter's brave journey on the sea, sometimes simply settling the spray of the crashing waves is not enough. Sometimes, we must step outside of the boat and allow the love of God to lap at our ankles as we wonder what in the earth we've gotten ourselves into. Other times, when the storm is fierce and frightening, all we have to do is remember who is in the boat with us, that God is not only expressed in the crashing waves, but also in Jesus asleep in the prow.

People who are hungry for revival need only pay attention to the ways the Holy Spirit is alive and active in our world and the ways in which our communal worship, though deceptively tame, is actually holding us afloat amid the powerful and overwhelming tide of God's grace that is transforming our world before our very eyes.

CHAPTER THREE

Come, Let Us Go

I was glad when they said to me, *
"Let us go to the house of the LORD."
Now our feet are standing *
within your gates, O Jerusalem.
Jerusalem is built as a city *
that is at unity with itself;
To which the tribes go up,
the tribes of the LORD, *
the assembly of Israel,
to praise the Name of the LORD.

(Psalm 122:1–4, BCP)

FOR SOME, CHURCH SMELLS LIKE THE STRONG ODOR of slightly bitter church coffee. For others, it is the smell of burning incense. For much of my life, it was the smell of spray starch mixed with the sweet scent of pancakes that reminded me most of church. Sunday mornings throughout my childhood were for church, but even before we joined with the other saints who were "glad to be in the House of the Lord one more time," there was a whole process of preparation.

It was a liturgy of sorts.

It began the night before when we'd set out our clothes. In my younger years the outfit was always a pair of khakis of various shades, a white shirt and tie, or a polo in the summer. The dress code relaxed a bit as I matured, for which I was grateful. While I am quite sure my brothers were dreading the next day, I was anticipating it. I fell in love with the whole idea of church and spirituality at a young age for reasons I am only now able to name. It might have something to do with a spacious "interior life," which I actively cultivated as an escape from the complicated emotions of growing up with few models for vulnerability and the fear of being different.

Sunday mornings always came quickly. They still do.

My mom and I would rise early, shower, iron our clothes, and head to church while the rest of my family slept. After the first "traditional" service, where the hymn choir would intone plaintive renditions of "Father I Stretch My Hands to Thee" and "Guide Me, O Thou Great Jehovah," we would come back home to retrieve the rest of the Halley clan, luring them from their beds with fresh pancakes (and sausage links if we were feeling fancy). They would rise, often begrudgingly, and perform the same ritual my mom and I had hours before. After ironing clothes and eating one too many pancakes, we'd load up in the family car and head to church for Sunday school, followed by worship, and then stay for lunch.

The memory of Sunday mornings is more than nostalgia for me. The way my mother taught me to prepare for church taught me something about its importance. This was not an ordinary thing we were doing. We were engaging in something that was fundamentally extraordinary and we were supposed to prepare for it as such. It was only recently that I have come to understand it as both an active participation in God's ongoing mission of reconciliation as well as an active participation in the vibrant life of the Holy Trinity. All I knew then was that something big was about to happen.

For my grandmother's generation, this always meant wearing your Sundays' best. The tradition of African Americans wearing their Sundays' best to church has its roots in slavery, when enslaved Africans would reserve their best clothes for Sunday service. In the throes of a dehumanizing system, slave religion provided enslaved Africans with the dignity often denied them by white people beyond the church community. This tradition continued post-emancipation, with free blacks wearing their Sundays' best almost as a protest against the dehumanization of Jim Crow segregation. In the Black Church, black women and men who often worked jobs considered menial by the larger, whiter society—jobs like seamstresses, maids, janitors, and bus drivers—were granted the dignity of being pastors, deacons and deaconesses, trustees, and ushers. Sunday's best was not simply about outward appearance. It was an affirmation of human dignity.

One of the first Episcopal liturgies my grandmother attended was my "first mass" as a newly ordained priest. She was bowled over by the grand architecture of the building, but was dismayed that people were wearing cargo shorts to church. "Don't they know who they are coming to see?" she asked. "They're coming to see the King." I had to explain to her the cultural difference that she was astutely noticing. I was also aware that she was coming from a context where preparing for Sunday worship was an ordeal, a labor of love, because what we were doing was nothing less than preparing to encounter the Sovereign of the Universe.

One of the things we can learn from our Jewish siblings is the reality that worship begins *before* we actually get to the place where worship happens. There is a whole division of the Psalms that contain the Songs of Ascent, the songs the faithful would sing as they journeyed up Mount Zion to the temple for worship. The Psalms, with rich phrases like "I lift up my eyes to the hills—from where will my help come?" and "I was glad when they said to me, 'Let us go to the house of the Lord!'" and "To you I lift up my eyes, O you who are enthroned in the heavens" make clear that the very act of going to worship was itself worship. Singing these songs on their way up God's holy hill was the Iron Age Jewish version of spraying too much spray starch on your khakis and managing to avoid spilling syrup on your shirt between services. It is a statement that what we are about to do is so groundbreaking that it has foreshocks.

When we prepare for worship with intention, we can experience the "foretaste of glory divine."

During my junior year of college, I decided to take a class on the Psalms. By this point in my life, I had an inkling that pursuing a graduate program in theology would follow and that, coupled with the fact that my Baptist upbringing had so immersed me in scripture that I was seduced into believing I knew it all, led me to do absolutely no reading for the class. I was able to get by for a few weeks by relying on the stored knowledge I had accumulated from over a decade of Sunday school classes, but eventually the material become more advanced. Before I knew it, I was behind and the class was moving so quickly and so deeply that it became increasingly impossible to catch up. By the time the class ended, I was barely hanging on, somehow managing to eke out a C. The professor, aware that I was imagining a future in theology and having tried several times to intervene, gave me one final warning. "If you want to remain where you are, do nothing. Growth and development require preparation."

Preparation and intention also go a long way in the spiritual life. Derek Olsen names "intentionality" as one of the disciplines necessary for us to "cooperate with God's transforming grace" brought about in our worship (*Inwardly Digest*, 41). We have to expect something to happen, to receive some insight, some glimpse into God's future, to find some new treasure or resource for courageous living that we thought we'd lost. And even if we don't get it, if we conclude our prayer only to find ourselves in the same space we were before we began, we must make expectation and discipline.

One of the unexpected gifts of a church in decline is that more and more, people are intentionally showing up for church looking for something, even if they cannot name it. Simply to get to church is to reject the narrative of a larger society that sees the worshiping community gathered around the Risen Christ as an obsolete relic of an unenlightened world. Worshipers have already said so many "yeses" to God before they arrive. What might it mean to make it an intentional practice to dig deeper, to bring to mind the reasons we show up? What if, on the journey to church, we named out loud how lonely we are and how much we hunger for the embrace of community, or how afraid we are and how much we need hope, or how our faith is on the verge of dying and just how much we need strength? What if we whispered a prayer that has become a mainstay of my spiritual life—God, help me. When we take time to engage the liturgy beforehand, becoming mindful of our hopes and fears, our blessings and our burdens, the whole endeavor can become immeasurably more meaningful.

It is deceptively easy to engage public liturgy the way I engaged my class on the Psalms. We have a body of knowledge about faith and our own experience that can sustain our journeys for a period, but after a while, we reap diminishing returns. Before long, our engagement with God through communal prayer becomes stilted and lifeless and, eventually, we find ourselves drifting away from the community Jesus tells us to remain close to. The Roman Catholic Church's *Constitution on the Sacred Liturgy*, published after the Second Vatican Council, sets high stakes for what happens in the community of faith on Sunday mornings. It says that "the liturgy is the summit toward which the activity of the Church is directed; at the same time it is the font from which all her power flows" (*Constitution of the Sacred Liturgy*, par. 10). Others have described our Sunday-keeping as the main repeated event that punctuates the course of our lives from the moment we are baptized until the moment we are taken into God's future.

There is a thought that the best thing the Church can and should do is feed the poor, shelter the unhoused, and liberate the prisoner. To be clear, the Church should be doing these things and, more importantly, empowering its members with the tools necessary to do this work in the world. However, this work lacks a focus unless we are lifted in our worship in a way that our sight is vastly expanded. In worship, we experience a prophetic vision—a glimpse into ever-adventing-but-not-quite-here reign of Christ. We are brought face-to-face with the God who created all things, who loves all that God has created, and who desires that we all experience the fullness of peace.

For Christians, there is nothing greater, nothing more loving, nothing of greater importance than worshiping God who is the fount of all creation. Everything we do and are is shaped by our worship and our proximity to the one who not only created us but draws us back to God's self in love. The love of God that draws us to worship also carries us into the world on a tide of grace. Worship and service are held in dynamic tension and the ebb and flow forms us as an instrument of peace and carriers of love. There is a story of an Eastern Orthodox priest who is asked, "Father, if God is everywhere, why do we have to come to church?" The priest responds, "The atmosphere is filled with water vapor, but if you wish to have a drink, you must come to well."

The well metaphor also opens up the possibility for us experiencing God's grace outside of the structure gathering of a Christian community, especially when we take into account artificial and naturally occurring wells. Once, while teaching a Confirmation preparation class, an astute confirmand asked me what a sacrament was. As any wise priest would, I directed them to "catechism" toward the back of the prayer book and had then read the definition of "sacrament" aloud:

The sacraments are outward and visible signs of inward and spiritual grace, given by Christ as sure and certain means by which we receive that grace. (BCP, 857)

After reading it through once, I had them read it again, stopping at the words "sure and certain." "Sacraments aren't the only place where we can receive God's grace," I said. "I bet if you think hard enough, you can think of a place outside of church where you experience God's love." They could. They began sharing moments when they felt supported by the drama club or sports team. A few students even shared about what it meant to experience God in the midst of their parents' divorce. When the groups' sharing came to a natural conclusion, I shared with them that the difference in sacraments in the life of Church and our experience of grace elsewhere comes down to faith. Beyond here, we are forced to rely on feelings and emotions, which are important, but not ultimate. In the life of faith, we trust that we are constantly being held in God's embrace, whether we can feel it or not. "Sure and certain" means that wherever else it may be, God's grace is definitely here.

The Church's understanding of the sacraments is firmly rooted in a theology of the Incarnation that challenges our perception of the way things are by consistently asking: If an infinite God can take on the finitude and fragility of the human form, where else might God unexpectedly show up?

Might God show up in bread and wine?

In water and oil?

In hands held in love?

In hands laid in power?

Words whispered in truth and heard in love?

Where two or three are gathered in the name of Jesus Christ?

One of the places it is hard to experience Christ is precisely in the crush of community. Leading communities of faith requires leaders to help individuals, and in some cases whole systems, to step beyond fear and anger and into a space of love and wholeness. This often requires having hard conversations. One such experience of this occurred when I had to have a conversation with someone who was accused of bullying people in a community I was leading. While his aggravating behavior had not reached the point of being abusive, as no one to my knowledge made that specific accusation, he was making it really difficult to be in community with him. I offered to meet with him over coffee to find out what was going on.

In the days leading up the meeting, I grew increasingly nervous about it. Hard conversations bring along with them a huge amount of risk and vulnerability. I was mindful of my own temptation toward vengeance when it came to perceived bullies, having been bullied in school. I was also aware that the only person I was in control of in that meeting was myself, that no matter how much I framed my words with love and support, I could not control his response. As we sat down for coffee, something dawned on me that frankly should dawn on me more often: *we should start the meeting with prayer.* After preparing myself for the feeling of embarrassment I still get whenever I pray in a public space that is not a church, I asked him if he would like to pray and after putting my hands on the table, palms up, in a sort of lazy "orans" position, I was surprised to see that he had reached his hands forward and we were holding hands. I am unsure what I prayed in that moment, but I do remember the first thing he said after we had concluded our prayer. "Thank you, Father. I probably should do that more."

He and I talked about his life, how his relationship with his adult children was estranged at best, how his own dark night of the soul never resolved itself and he wasn't quite sure what to make of all this "Jesus stuff," how he loved the parish community but never seemed to land anywhere meaningful. "I guess I am just trying to find where I belong."

I know that feeling. Like Harry Potter's lightning-shaped scar which throbbed with pain whenever he came near to "he who shall not be named," I have my own scar, one that throbs whenever I hear someone talk about not belonging or feeling silenced. I had been on the receiving end of this man's passive-aggressive e-mails, his aggravating behavior, and his unhelpful and mean-spirited criticism, but I realized that it was coming from somewhere deep within that lacked the language to name his true feelings. He was hurt and could not bring himself to name it. I listened to him share his story, to whatever degree he could, as a holy act within a holy space. I thought I was going in to reprimand him. I walked away having met Christ in his scars.

In the summer of 1941, C. S. Lewis gave a sermon called "The Weight of Glory," exploring the ways that God's glory transforms us into new creations. He closes this sermon by inviting the listener to recognize the incredible holiness of another person.

> There are no *ordinary* people. You have never talked to a mere mortal. Nations, cultures, arts, civilization—these are mortal, and their life is to ours as the life of a gnat. But it is immortals whom we joke with, work with, marry, snub, and exploit—immortal horrors or everlasting splendors. This does not mean that we are to be perpetually solemn. We must play. But our merriment must be of that kind (and it is, in fact, the merriest kind) which exists between people who have, from the outset, taken each other seriously—no flippancy, no superiority, no presumption. And our charity must be a real and costly love, with deep feeling for the sins in spite of which we love the sinner—no mere tolerance, or indulgence which parodies love as flippancy parodies merriment. Next to the Blessed Sacrament itself, your neighbor is the holiest object presented to your senses. (Lewis, *Weight of Glory*, 46)

Throughout this sermon, Lewis invites his listeners to something deeper and more profound than a mere surface engagement with religion and relationships. God has done nothing less than share divine grace with us in such a way that we are called to a radical re-visioning of one another. If holiness can be found in the Blessed Sacrament and in the existence of another, what might it look like to take this seriously, to prepare for an encounter across significant cultural difference with intention, anticipation, and humility? What might it mean to cultivate the space to go into a tough conversation remembering that the person with whom we are speaking is created in the same divine image as we are?

Our society seems to have forgotten this and seems to be relishing in the amnesia. Our divisive politics reveal that we seem less and less interested in constructing coalitions across differences and less interested in increasing our capacity for imagination in ways that enable the construction of new communities and the reshaping of relationships. We seem committed to an endless volleying of power back and forth, creating an endless cycle of winners and losers, rather than engaging in the hard, relational work Jesus asks of us in the gospel, work that invites us to transcend the politics of power that define our present age in order to bear witness to the in-breaking reign of God.

This is not to suggest that we are not to be involved politically in every way that we can. The idea that we can somehow exist in the world apolitically is a fallacy that causes great harm to those who are the most vulnerable in our society. Not to speak, not to participate, is itself a politic, and one that reflects an immense level of privilege. What would it mean to participate politically in a way that resembles Jesus? What if we understood the politics of Jesus to be neither left nor right nor mythical center, but something altogether different? What might it mean to leverage relationships to bring about change rather than merely snatching power from those we see as our opponents? What might it mean to see humanity before we see difference, even when that benefit of the doubt is not extended to us? What might it mean to do this with a posture of humility, fully realizing that everything we do will fall short of the kingdom of God because that is not what we are building. We are seeking to build a just, sustainable, compassionate, and free society that nurtures the human spirit and one day all of that will dissolve before the fullness of God's reign. I am not suggesting that this is in any way easy. It is certainly not. I do know that we have to begin trying on new skills to relate across our political spectrum or else risk solidifying these political differences for future generations, diminishing their ability to bring about change in their time.

It is easy to borrow aspects of Jesus to craft a particular political narrative. To a certain degree we all do this. I have become curious of late of the parts of Jesus's message that I am wont to avoid, particularly the parts that ask me to do something that costs me something. Toward the beginning of Matthew's Gospel, the Evangelist has Jesus delivering what is probably his most famous public address, the Sermon on the Mount. Toward the middle of his address, probably right when Jesus was feeling reasonably comfortable with his audience, he delivers this zinger:

> You have heard that it was said, "You shall love your neighbor and hate your enemy." But I say to you, Love your enemies and pray for those who persecute you, so that you may be children of your Father in heaven; for he makes his sun rise on the evil and on the good, and sends rain on the righteous and on the unrighteous. For if you love those who love you, what reward do you have? Do not even the tax collectors do the same? And if you greet only your brothers and sisters, what more are you doing than others? Do not even the Gentiles do the same? Be perfect, therefore, as your heavenly Father is perfect. (Matt. 5:43–48)

Elsewhere in the gospels, Jesus is quoted as saying "love your neighbor" and "love one another," but only here (and in Luke's "Sermon on the Plain") does the Bible record Jesus as saying "love your enemy." It might be tempting to assume that these three statements are saying the same thing. They could not be more different. When Jesus was talking about the love of neighbor and loving "one another," he was leaning heavily into his Jewish identity. According to Amy-Jill Levine, Jewish law required all Jews to love those within the community, love that especially manifested itself in action with and toward the most vulnerable. When it came to enemies, one was not allowed to mistreat them, but neither was one commanded to "love" them in the same way that one was commanded to love their neighbors—both those in Jewish community and non-Jewish people who lived in close proximity. "Only Jesus insists on loving the enemy," she writes. "He may be the only person in antiquity to have given this instruction" (Levine, *Short Stories of Jesus*, 86).

Love of the enemy was a new innovation in the time of Christ, and one we haven't quite gotten down just yet. To love an enemy requires the imaginative capacity to reshape the relationship between offender and offended, oppressor and oppressed, powerful and the powerless. To love an enemy requires that we reshape power dynamics and structure new ways of being together. Activist and organizer adrienne maree brown asks an incisive question in her book *Emergent Strategy*, "When we imagine the world we want to shift towards, are we dreaming of being the winners of the future? Or are we dreaming of a world where winning is no longer necessary because there are no enemies?" (*Emergent Strategy*, 132). The world that Jesus dreams of—the kingdom of God—is a world where winning is no longer necessary because there are no enemies.

And we aren't there yet.

I've experienced the tug that exists between the aspiration and our lived reality in many places throughout the Church. There are places where the Church has sought to redress wrong and heal harm caused by racism and white supremacy, sexism and gender bias, heteronormativity and homophobia, and there are places where deep distrust still exists among those who have been negatively impacted by institutional oppression. There are still enemies, even in the church, because we are still learning how to transform our relationships beyond the seemingly intractable network of pain we have inherited. The powerful are still learning what it means to cede power while the powerless often struggle with the vulnerability of trying on power in a system that is still tooled for old relationships.

Once, after I had made a comment about my experience as a gay Christian in a sermon, a man and his wife sent a series of e-mails and passive-aggressive prayers to myself and the other members of the clergy of our parish. These prayers were placed in our mailboxes, taped to the sacristy door, and in one case slipped into my hand while we were shaking hands at the end of the liturgy. It was early enough in my priesthood that it felt like a personal attack, but late enough that I had learned how to transcend anger and offense by adopting a stance of curiosity. Rather than retreat from the relationship, I decided to lean in by inviting them into a conversation. It was hard, but I worked to retain a stance of curiosity and wonder.

As we spoke, he shared with me something that I had forgotten since coming out of the closet. We both shared an affinity for scripture, even if we had come to interpret it very differently. The Bible shaped both our worldviews in profound ways. The difference was that he had been taught to read the Bible in a way that caused him to view people who identify as LGBTQ+ as inherently sinful and in need of God's grace. I had learned that way of reading scripture as well, but gave it up when I realized it was harming me. I didn't get there overnight. It took years of prayer and study for me to get to a place where I saw God's love for me reflected in scripture. I am grateful for all the people who were patient with me as I engaged that transformation for myself, from teachers and therapists to priests and friends. From that awareness, I was able to connect with the reality that for him to veer from that understanding was impossible in that moment. "This is not about you," he told me. "This is about me living my faith in a way that I think pleases God."

I did not then, nor do I now, agree with him. LGBTQ folks are wholly beloved by God just as we are and we bear the responsibility, as do all human beings, of engaging our sexuality in ways that are healthy, holy, and life-giving. I also disagree with the idea that him living his faith in a way that he thought would please God gave him license to inflict harm on me or others. Any type of Christian faith that seeks to impose itself on another in the name of grace represents a fundamental misunderstanding of grace. Where I could join him was when he talked about how the Bible had shaped his life. I know what it feels like to be held close to something that shapes you so profoundly it is next to impossible to imagine a life without it.

This encounter showed me the power of compassion and what might happen if we engaged most issues from a place of curiosity. To my knowledge, we still disagree about this issue to this very day. What that encounter changed for me was not my perspective but my posture. It is a vulnerable place, but I found myself able to hold him accountable for respecting a boundary and also see him as a flawed human being. What I was fighting in that moment, and continue to fight, is not really an individual, but a system that invites people into such a harmful view of God. I am still learning to see people not as opponents and the space between us as a sparse "no man's land," but as siblings sharing one Creator and the space between us as holy and fertile.

That requires the same preparation we might apply to preparing for worship. In one another, we experience the presence of Christ. When that relationship is defined by brokenness, mistrust, and harm, learning to see that space as holy might be helpful. Even in situations where reconciliation is next to impossible, what might it mean to hallow that space anyway, to open our hearts to curiosity, to keep our souls open to never-ending threat of Easter?

I ran a small liturgical experiment one summer when worship attendance falls in half as people spend the summer months traveling. I decided to begin worship with asking people to breathe deeply, feel themselves grounded in the space, and set an intention for their worship practice that day. "What do you need?" I asked. "Do you need peace? Joy? Confidence? Forgiveness? Love? Ask for it and keep your intention with you during our practice this morning." When I got pushback, I discovered that many folks were triggered by how close and intimate it felt. They knew that God loved "the world," but they had never really been given permission to consider God's love for them and their stuff—mundane and major. After a while, people settled into the new practice, becoming increasingly comfortable with asking God for what they needed.

There have been times in my own life—times when my "imposter syndrome" is at full flame or when I feel particular lonely—when I am forced to cry out "God, help!" But what if this practice wasn't merely born of desperation, but was something I practiced on a regular basis? What if I believed in my worthiness enough and in God's love enough to ask God for what I needed? What if the entire time I was preparing for worship I was whispering a prayer:

God, I don't feel like I deserve to be doing this. Please give me confidence.

Dear Jesus, I am tired and the world sucks. Give me patience and resilience.

Dear God . . . you already know. I need you.

And what if we took that same practice into our lives, asking for what we needed from allies, coworkers, family members, friends, and colleagues? What if we prepared for hard conversations by holding reconciliation as an intention? What if we dared to believe that God was still capable of bringing beauty from our ashes and joy from our pain if we were just aware of our need for it and brave enough to ask for it?

My grandmother's belief in the power of God is connected to her belief that God's love has bearing on every part of her life. Everything from physical pain to the death of loved ones to the fragile status of the world is of incredible concern to God. As I heard her sing more than once:

> What a friend we have in Jesus,
> all our sins and griefs to bear.
> What a privilege to carry
> everything to God in prayer.
> O, what peace we often forfeit,
> O, what needless pain we bear,
> all because we do not carry
> everything to God in prayer.
>
> (Joseph Scriven, "What a Friend We Have in Jesus,"
> *African American Heritage Hymnal*, 431)

A deep relationship with Christ and reconciled relationships with others both require the same thing: intention. We have to prepare for the future we desire and then make choices in that direction even if that direction takes us up a rocky hill.

Because what we seek isn't just at the top. It is experienced in each small, stumbling step we take.

CHAPTER FOUR

Gather in the Lord's Name

When the day of Pentecost had come, they were all together in one place. And suddenly from heaven there came a sound like the rush of a violent wind, and it filled the entire house where they were sitting. Divided tongues, as of fire, appeared among them, and a tongue rested on each of them. All of them were filled with the Holy Spirit and began to speak in other languages, as the Spirit gave them ability.

(Acts 2:1–4)

FAMILY REUNIONS IN MY FAMILY were times to come together and remember. I suspect that is true for most families. In my younger years, my family lived relatively close to one another, so the need for a regular and intentional family reunion was minimal. At one point, we lived next door to an aunt, behind a cousin, across town from other relatives, and one town removed from my grandmother. Geography and proximity made "family reunions" pointless. Sunday afternoons were family reunions by default, with the whole family filling the modest homes of my maternal grandmother or one of her siblings. That changed once we began to move away from New Jersey, with the adults drawn to the South for a lower cost of living or pursuing employment opportunities. It was after a few years of living apart from our close-knit family that my mother first got the idea of organizing a family reunion.

They were by no means elaborate affairs. For most of it, we would simply recreate what we did before we all moved away—we'd gather in my grandmother's house for dinner, share stories, hear about the latest drama, and love each other anyway. When I think about the incredible simplicity of these gatherings, I remember a TedTalk given by Nigerian novelist Chiamanda Adichie on "The Danger of a Single Story." Adichie's talk expounds on the power of storytelling in shaping our own world, and on how we see and experience the world of another.

She concludes her talk by referencing a story from Alice Walker. Walker's family, like many black families in the early to mid-1900s, made the great trek from the American South to places like New York and New Jersey, Chicago, and Los Angeles, fleeing racial violence and in search of new job prospects. When she shared with them a book they had left behind about the South, she says that "they sat around, reading the book themselves, listening to me read the book, and a kind of paradise was regained" (Adiche, *https://www.ted.com/talks/chimamanda_ngozi_adichie_the_danger_of_a_single_story?language=en*, 17:53). There is something incredibly powerful about the gathering of any dispersed community, especially a community that experiences displacement. The simple act of gathering, or remembering, quite literally puts the pieces back together.

During one particular family reunion, after the family had eaten and had made their way out to my grandmother's backyard, her brother, Uncle Sonnyboy, sat down in a lawn chair and began to share stories. Without even issuing an invitation or command, the individual members of my family simply began gathering around my great-uncle as he sat in a green lawn chair. His stories opened a new world to us. He shared stories of the time he, as a child, integrated a train car while he, his siblings, and his mother were traveling from New Jersey to South Carolina. He also talked about his parents—both children of sharecroppers—who managed to eke out a life together in the middle of Jim Crow segregation. I am clear that some of his stories were more true than others. Lore plays an important role in how any group chooses to remember and know themselves. The details of these stories never seemed terribly important to him. What was most important is that we understood our gathering as more than simply a get-together. For my great-uncle, gathering as a family helped us to remember our own identity as a people.

People gather. It's kind of our thing. In many of her books on leadership and vulnerability, Brené Brown talks about the degree to which human beings are made for authentic connection. "Hiding out, pretending, and armoring up against vulnerability are killing us: killing our spirits, our hopes, our potential, our creativity, our ability to lead, our love, our faith, and our joy" (*Rising Strong*, xix). There seems to be something woven into the fabric of humanity that yearns to be a part of something beyond ourselves. One of the ways the hardwiring manifests itself is in the way that we gather and sort ourselves into different communities. Neighborhood associations, civic groups, church committees, book clubs, community choirs, all of these are examples of humans gathering and sorting themselves. This can even be seen at any coffee shop. Notice the number of people who are sitting alone, working, or writing. There has even been an increase in coworking organizations, where people can work independently but still benefit from the synergy that happens when human beings gather. Even in moments when we want to be "alone," we seem to want to be alone *in community*.

The identity and values of any community are expressed in how they gather. When I was a Boy Scout, we began each troop meeting with an elaborate ritual that held up the values of our community. After assembling in our patrols, we'd raise the American flag and say the Pledge of Allegiance before reciting the Scout Oath and the Scout Law. From the onset of any meeting, the community was reminded that our identity as Boy Scouts was expressed in duty to our country, to our fellow scouts, and to our community.

Gathering reveals the identity of any group.

When I think about what it means to gather as Christians, my mind takes an imaginative journey back to the earliest days of the Church, before we had widespread consensus on set rites and rituals, before canons and committees, when communities of Jesus followers would gather in synagogues and then gather in homes, in catacombs, in the wilderness, to share stories and break bread, to reaffirm their commitment to Torah, and to reconnect to their new identity in Christ. That they gathered at all says something about what it means to be a follower of Christ, that it is impossible to follow Christ without some kind of community. This is likely hard to hear in a time when a growing number of people are identifying as "spiritual but not religious," but part-and-parcel with following the Risen One is a connection to the community that bears his name.

This is difficult, especially when some of the Church's struggles to know and affirm marginalized people have resulted in trauma and rejection for so many. A truth we have to name is the number of people who deal with some very real pain associated with the Church. The Church has not always been welcoming and affirming of people of color, LGBTQ+ folks, women, those with physical disabilities, and others. Indeed, we still have work to do in each of these areas and more. If, as some argue, the body processes emotional pain, like rejection, as a physical experience, then being rejected from a community such as the Church can feel like abuse and betrayal. There are many folks whose journey with the Church has come to an end—at least through traditional avenues—because of the ways the Church has failed to live into its identity as the body of Christ, the body whose very scars show solidarity with the suffering of our own day. An ongoing challenge of the Church will be figuring out how to communicate the power of the Christian faith through unconventional avenues to reach the sheep we lost in our infighting and lack of compassion.

I remember my own experience of exile after I advocated for LGBTQ+ folks in my childhood congregation. The reaction was swift. I was out. I had a conversation with a church planter who identifies as gay some years after that experience. I wanted to see if his experience of church planting could shed some light on my own vocational rumblings. Shortly into the conversation he remarked that "queer Christians have always been church planters by default." I was intrigued by this comment and pressed him for more. "The institution didn't want us, but our souls longed for grace, so we created the kinds of communities we needed, communities where we not only felt grace but could lavish it on others who share our wounds."

He was right. His words reminded me of my own hardwiring for community and longing for the cooling waters of grace. Throughout my life, even before I knew that I was gay or felt that I had permission to name it, I was creating communities with others who shared my wounds. I had organized Bible studies in college, queer-affirming chapel services in seminary, and was sought out for counsel by LGBTQ+ members of a church made up of people experiencing homelessness. I don't know that anyone "called" me to do this work. I just did it because I needed it and I knew that there were others who needed it too.

Still, that experience of expulsion hurt so deeply because it was rejection by a community that I held so dear, the community that nurtured me, first identified my own call to ministry, supported my dreams by sitting through quite a few terrible sermons, even giving me a few "amens" to support my journey. While I connected to another spiritual home almost immediately after having to leave my former one, it took a few years for me to learn to trust the community again. In many aspects, I am still learning to trust Christian community. That experience taught me that trust is born by showing up again and again and discovering that what you fear the most is untrue.

Somehow, we have to undo the damaging self-assumption that we are perfect, that our faith communities shot up out of the ground full grown. Christians can be good at telling you where they are but are often unwilling to name the journey that got them there. I have spent my life in Christian communities of varying types and sizes—large, evangelical megachurches; small, black Baptist congregations; storefronts; campus chapels; and almost everything in between—and not one of them has been perfect. I have often wondered what the value might be for Christian communities to claim their imperfection, to name explicitly the places where they struggle, to follow the example of our Risen Lord and show the world our scars and then invite the world to come closer, to engage with us as the tender, beautifully broken community we actually are.

A few years ago, members of my congregation were looking at church websites to get some ideas for how we might better talk about ourselves as a community. What we noticed on each website was that each church led with what it perceived to be its strengths. Churches with huge programs for young families with children had pictures of children all over their website. Churches with great choral programs filled their websites with images of choristers in red robes and Elizabethan collars. Communities with demonstrated commitment to engaging with their communities through social justice and advocacy had pictures of parishioners holding up placards at a march or bending over to wash the feet of those who were homeless. I get it. Churches grow from their strengths. It's Isaac Newton's Law of Motion—an object in motion will tend to stay in motion. A church with a huge cohort of young children is likely to continue to attract people who desire that type of church experience.

But I wonder, in a time when more and more people struggle with anxiety, depression, and hopelessness, who is being left out as we lead with our strengths. Most churches I visit claim to be welcoming to all, but very few allocate resources to non-English-speaking worshipers, accommodate people with physical disabilities, or have any bandwidth for worship that deviates from a specific cultural norm. In addition to all these areas of potential growth, every congregation has some story of trauma and grace because human gathering is risky and messy. These traumatic experiences are found in the stories old-timers share during coffee hour when the new priest isn't around or in the cold relationships that exist between long-term members. What might it mean to tell the truth, to name to those who are seeking a spiritual home that we are an imperfect community committed to following the way of Jesus the best we can? What if, instead of churches simply claiming to be affirming of LGBTQ+ folks, we named that the journey to this reality was hard, that we had to grow and change in order to get to this place, that we have still more growing to do in order to be what we desire to be? What if, instead of claiming to be committed multiracial and multiethnic faith communities, we told the stories of how much our communities benefited from white supremacy and what work we're doing to repair the damage?

If it sounds scary, it should.

Bearing witness to Jesus Christ should be a little scary or else we might want to ask who it is that we are really following. To borrow from Rowan Williams, Christians are found in the neighborhood of Jesus and Jesus seems to always find himself in the neighborhood of risk. I don't have evidence that this will change anything, I just know that in a world where projections of pride and power are yielding destruction, vulnerability and honesty might be a way forward. In a world where too many spaces require too many of us to wear a shield of armor, good news might look like cultivating authentic communities where we can take our armor off for a little while. The world is yearning for truthful, vulnerable relationships that break us out of the technological malaise and social isolation that affects so many of us. We yearn to be in the "sweaty, intimate, flesh-and-blood embrace" that Rachel Held Evans talks about in *Searching for Sunday*. We yearn for something that pulls us into a different reality than so many of us experience on a daily basis.

That we *still* gather at all as a messy, fragile community says something about us. *When* we gather says a whole lot more.

One of the first rituals around which the early Christian communities coalesced was the keeping of Sunday. At first, Jewish Christians gathered in homes after the Friday night Shabbat services in the synagogue. Eventually, Christians began to increasingly identify with the resurrection and thus began to keep the Sunday feast. Before there were commemorations of Easter or Christmas, Christians gathered to participate in the unremittingness of Sunday after Sunday after Sunday. Time is marked and sanctified by sharing in the rhythm of Sunday observance. It's a journey that throws off the temptation of spirituality-on-demand or instant gratification. A life in Christ marked by countless Sundays is a life committed to slow sanctification that happens when I regularly offer more and more of myself to Christ until Christ is truly my "all in all."

I understand how terrible this sounds to people committed to the life a culture of acquisitiveness demands of us—endless work with little to no periods of true rest that work together to create an identity based on one's ability to produce. To stop, to demand that our lives be defined not by production but by Christ, to offer ourselves not to a dehumanizing system that monetizes us but into the grace of God who loves us, to admit to ourselves that wonderful though we might be, we are not perfect and we are in need of a Savior to set us free from the life-diminishing rat race over and over again is a huge leap.

And it's the leap that Christ asks of us.

Nothing breaks my heart quite like the apathy or powerlessness that people demonstrate when they claim a commitment to Christ but only gather in community once-a-month or so. If you ever want to become aware of the sinfulness of our economic system, look not only to how the poor are treated with such contempt, but look at how many folks are slaves to a dehumanizing and exploitative system. It seems inescapable. It's not simply that I want people to come to church. If church were merely a gathering of people coming together to sing songs, share a bizarre table ritual, and hear fantastical stories, I'd just as soon stay home like everyone else.

Our gathering is so much more. A gathering of Christians is by definition more than the sum of our parts. Our Lord promises that where two or three of his disciples gather, he will be in the midst of us. This depth of meaning is made infinitely deeper when we add sacraments to the mix. The multiple layers of meaning that collide in the meeting of any gathering of Christians speaks to the incredible depth of the life that is possible when we expose our world-weary souls to it over and over and over again. I want people to experience the depth of life that is possible when we claim a resurrection identity over that of a consumer identity. I likewise want people to experience "the love of Christ that surpasses knowledge, so that [they] may be filled with all the fullness of God" (Eph. 3:19). Bishop J. Neil Alexander writes that "[Episcopalians] are wired for the long haul; a journey from font to eternity that is punctuated by a thousand successive Sundays that carry us forward with the inexhaustible energy of Resurrection" ("On Sacraments and Sundays" in *Common Prayer*, 20). Life becomes so much richer when we are made aware of all the ways God's future and all of salvation history come crashing together when Christians gather in the name of Jesus Christ.

It is no mistake that my family grew up going to church each Sunday. It was a practice that had been handed to us through countless generations of faithful Christians who were clear that either our ultimate identity is found in Christ or we are utterly lost. This heavenward identity bore up the souls of my ancestors whose bodies were beaten and worn down by the brutality of slavery in America. It is the heavenward identity that many LGBTQ+ Christians like myself claim even amid those who would say that our identities and our faith are inherently in conflict. Despite the attempts of the powerful, the marginalized always seem to stretch forward through the veil of eternity, dragging the kingdom of God into the present. This is both a warning and an invitation. First, we are warned to be on guard for any attempt within ourselves to deny this heavenward identity in others lest we lose sight of our own. Second, we are invited to wonder about the work God is doing when marginalized folks demand seats at the tables of the powerful. It might be that they are there to bring the kingdom of God from the place it is most likely to hang out—with those of whom Jesus says, "Blessed are they."

If Christians are to have anything of value to say to the world, we must do so rooted firmly in the nurturing soil of resurrection. Love of neighbor, service to and advocacy alongside the poor, and dismantling unjust systems all have inherent value, and they carry even more weight and import when we understand this activity as participating in the dawning of a new age. If all we have to offer the world is righteous anger and baptized pop psychology, then we have nothing to offer except an endless cycle of violence and death. Our work as disciples has an end—the reign of Christ. The Christian witness ceases to be authentically Christian if it is not connected to the movement that bears his name and if we are not standing with both feet planted firmly in the new age brought about by his resurrection. Christians aren't simply called to make the world a better place. That work might sound good, but it is ultimately too small. It bears repeating that Jesus did not come to make the world *better*. He came to make all things *new*. Through our ministry, we are called to bear out the reality that the world is being made new by God who has already done the heavy lifting and is simply inviting us to join the movement.

Last summer, a friend who was serving as a deacon in my congregation was ordained a priest before moving to Maine. I wrestled for a while to think of a gift to give her as she began her new journey serving God's Church as a priest. Her journey, like so many young women I know pursuing ordination, was long and fraught with many challenges and setbacks. The gift idea came to me when I was with the seminary community in Chapel of the Apostles during a summer program at Sewanee. When I was there, there was one icon over the ambo—the *Anastasis* or "Resurrection." Since I left as a seminarian, two more have been added, Pentecost and the Holy Myrrh Bearers. I was drawn to the latter, to this icon of the three women going to the tomb of Jesus post-resurrection. They are carrying their spices because they are expecting death. But when they arrive, they find an angel sitting atop the tomb, the tomb open, and the grave clothes empty inside. I thought about the power of that singular moment in history and about how, even though the resurrection of Jesus Christ is a historic event, its effects are still present in the world today. After all, the Easter acclamation is in the present tense: "Alleluia! Christ *is* risen!" I managed to find a copy of the icon and before I mailed it to her, I wrote this on the back of it: *everything is different now.*

The Church is a gathering of imperfect people trying as best we can to live the way of Jesus Christ and sometimes we get that really wrong. We harm people in our anger. We are selfish. We are stubborn. We don't listen well. We insist on our way or the highway. We are quick to critique and slow to forgive. God knows we can be filled with fear and anxiety in the face of change. If not for the love of Christ and the power of his resurrection, I would've thrown in the towel the moment a white parishioner sent me an e-mail that said, "Remember, this is our church, not yours." It is precisely because of the Resurrection, because God's future is adventing upon us in the present, because the reign of Christ is at hand, that I can wake up each day to follow the path to which God has called me. Talking about the freedom in Christ that propels him forward in his ministry, Paul the Apostle says, "I want to know Christ and the power of his resurrection and the sharing of his sufferings by becoming like him in his death, if somehow I may attain the resurrection from the dead" (Phil. 3:10–11). Awareness of the power of the resurrection at work in us gives our work an end and a goal—the reign of Christ. Though we will not experience it in its fullness on this side of death or the Second Coming, it is raining down upon us everywhere we look.

It is the love of Christ and the power of his resurrection that sustains us when the world is spinning out of control, when our collective addiction to violence, slavery to consumerism, indifference toward the well-being of the earth, and callousness toward human suffering threatens to undo our very humanity. It is the love of Christ and the power of his resurrection that gives motion and trajectory to our weary feet when we are marching to protect the rights of the vulnerable or protest the abuses of the powerful. It is the love of Christ and the power of his resurrection that animates our hands as we reach out in compassion to the suffering and lonely. It is the love of Christ and the power of his resurrection that enables our eyes to see the brokenness of this world and to respond with grace and conviction that the way things are is not the way they have to be. It is the love of Christ and the power of his resurrection that opens our hearts to the hard work of forgiveness and reconciliation when old ways of relating to one another prove incapable of bearing up transforming relationships.

We do all of this, not simply because they are compassionate things to do, but because we see a new world is breaking through right now, that the mighty are being cast down, that the poor are being raised up, that the rich are being sent away empty and the hungry are being filled. We do what we do as followers of Jesus because we live in a new age, one in which compassion, not enmity, rules the day. We do what we do because *Christ is risen and everything is different now!*

Though this prayer is only used a few times during the year in the Episcopal Church—mostly at the ordinations and consecrations of clergy and during Good Friday and Easter Vigil—it is a prayer that I believe speaks to weekly rhythm of the Christian life:

> O God of unchangeable power and eternal light: Look favorably on your whole Church, that wonderful and sacred mystery; by the effectual working of your providence, carry out in tranquility the plan of salvation; let the whole world see and know that things which were cast down are being raised up, and things which had grown old are being made new, and that all things are being brought to their perfection by him through whom all things were made, your Son Jesus Christ our Lord. *Amen.* (BCP, 291)

We gather to bear witness to the astonishing reality—the new-making of God. Everything that comes after we gather bears out

and fleshes out the whole reason why we are here—to become witnesses not simply of the resurrection as a historical event, but the resurrection *now*.

Whether we gather with an organ voluntary and opening acclamation, praise and worship and an invocation, or a moment of quiet
and deep listening before an information greeting; whether we gather
in a grand cathedral, a whitewashed chapel, a storefront, or on the
sidewalk; whether there are hundreds or a handful; whether or not
the choir is present or the senior minister is on vacation, when we
gather as a community in Christ on Sundays, we are bearing witness
to something spectacular—the ongoing appropriation of the resurrection. When we get up on a Sunday morning and gather ourselves
and our families for worship, we are making a statement about the
power of the resurrection in our own lives. When we join the Christian faithful from across the world and gather on the Lord's Day to
worship God "in spirit and in truth," we push back against the narrative that God is dead, that we are trapped in devastation and disaster,
that we are slaves to a dehumanizing economic system, that there is
no hope for a new world. Simply by gathering, we show the world
that there is a community of folks committed to experiencing and
sharing the power of the resurrection.

In a time when we are being driven more and more toward isolation and division, gathering at all is revolutionary. Gathering on
Sunday around the Risen Christ is even more revolutionary. It affirms
the Lordship of Christ even as the petty potentates of our age reveal
the fragility of all earthly nations and kingdoms. Our gathering also
invites people to be a part of more than a community—something
they can likely find elsewhere. It invites people into a more profound
reality of truth that saturates every day with infinite meaning because
every day is merely days away from Sunday.

And our gathering is merely the beginning.

CHAPTER FIVE

Proclaim and Respond to the Word of God

I shall continue to keep your law; *
    I shall keep it for ever and ever.
I will walk at liberty, *
    because I study your commandments.
I will tell of your decrees before kings *
    and will not be ashamed.
I delight in your commandments, *
    which I have always loved.
I will lift up my hands to your commandments, *
    and I will meditate on your statutes.

(Ps. 119:44–48, BCP)

UNTIL RECENTLY, if I were to describe my relationship with the Bible on Facebook, it would have been classified as "it's complicated."

I grew up in a Christian tradition that loved the Bible, and in fact, much of my love for scripture was cultivated in my earliest years. The Sunday school of my youth began with children reciting their memorized verses of scripture from the previous week and closed with a verse to memorize for the following week. Youth group games often centered around who could find the Bible verse first. Sermons were filled with invitations to "turn in your Bibles to . . ." and litany of scripture citations to look up once we got home. We also carried our Bibles to church with us lest we be viewed as the heathens—or visitors—who had to use the pew Bible. This incredibly rigorous biblical education served me well, and the more I read scripture, the more I fell in love with the God of whom it spoke. By the time I saw the Bible used as a weapon, I had bought into its inerrant authority hook, line, and sinker.

And that betrayal of trust hurt like hell.

My relationship with the Bible has often been complicated, but it never got to the point of divorce. Even at its most fraught, I still felt like Peter when Jesus asked him and the other eleven disciples if they were going to follow the others and desert him. "Lord, to whom can we go? You have the words of eternal life" (John 6:68). Beneath all the hard scriptures, I knew that there was something about this book that pointed to the new life that I had experienced in Christ. I also knew that there was something about this book that defined the Christian community in a unique way. I knew that being a Christian, being a follower of Jesus, meant engaging with the Bible in some way. Motivated more by desperation than faithfulness, I fought to reclaim the power and blessing of the Bible in my life as a gay person. It had once been life to me, and I knew that it could be again.

Proclaiming and responding to the Word of God is something Christians do when we gather. Whatever else we are, we are a people who are brought together by invitation to participate with God in the telling of the stories of God's mighty acts. One of the most compelling pieces of scripture—one that regularly resurfaces in my mind—is the passage from Deuteronomy where Moses is instructing the people of Israel not to forget all that they had been through, all that they had seen, and all they had been taught. It is one thing to hold on to God when God's promise was off in the distance, but they were about to go in to the Promised Land. As Walter Brueggemann puts it, "Moses knew that prosperity breeds amnesia" (Brueggemann, *Sabbath as Resistance*, 37). The antidote to forgetfulness is storytelling as a part of communal ritual.

> You shall put these words of mine in your heart and soul, and you shall bind them as a sign on your hand, and fix them as an emblem on your forehead. *Teach them to your children*, talking about them when you are at home and when you are away, when you lie down and when you rise. Write them on the doorposts of your house and on your gates, so that your days *and the days of your children* may be multiplied in the land that the Lord swore to your ancestors to give them, as long as the heavens are above the earth. (Deut. 11:18–21, emphasis added)

Telling stories is directly connected to retaining the blessing of God—demonstrated here in their days being multiplied. The idea that the people of God are called to remember and pass on is not new. As with most children, I went through a pretty rough adolescence. The transition from childhood to adulthood is never easy, especially for those navigating developing identities that do not conform to normative standards of sexuality. Once, after being suspended from school, my grandmother sat me down. I thought she was going to scold me or tell me how terrible a grandchild I was. Instead, she simply began telling me the stories of my family—stories of my great-grandmother Catherine who worked as a maid to provide for her family, stories of my great-grandfather George Buster who worked for an oil company that took him away from his family for months at a time, stories of how education was the tool used by my family to make a better life for themselves. The message was clear, even if left unsaid: education is important—too important to waste on anger and disrespectful behavior. Hearing the stories of my family served in that moment as a corrective for behavior that had fallen beneath the standard my family expected of me.

In a time when so many individuals are experiencing a sense of spiritual and emotional displacement, I wonder about the need not only to reclaim stories as sources for identity, community, and belonging but also to find and pay attention to new sources for cultural stories. The Me Too and Black Lives Matter movements as well as the ongoing development of our understanding of human sexuality are among the new sources that we are being invited to pay attention to. They seem to be tearing at the fabric of our cultural identity, and rightly so, especially since our cultural identity failed to tell the whole truth. The past few years have seen the shredding of a few powerful cultural narratives that were based on a revisionist history or outright lies. When Native people rightly challenge our broader understanding of the founding of the United States and when African Americans, Chinese Americans, and other people of color challenge the narrative of freedom and ingenuity, unless we are intentional about creating and adopting a new national story, we are left without a compelling story for our collective identity. The result is either nihilistic pessimism or stubborn entrenchment. Our society is filled with both.

I wonder about what it might mean to take history seriously, to dig into the stories of our nation's founding as complicated, and bloody, and oppressive as well as idealistic, and hopeful, and visionary. What might it mean to hold all these truths in a complex tension and allow them to teach us something not only about who we were and who we are, but who we might yet be? What if the monuments we raised above city squares and traffic circles told the whole truth of who we are as a nation, not simply the parts of the story we often like to remember with a certain amount of ahistorical nostalgia. If scripture is any guide in this area, the only way we can claim the blessing of God on ourselves and on our children is by passing on stories that tell the truth and grant us a moral framework for living.

The power of a story to convey the soul of a community is unmatched. The first thing I do when I arrive as a new clergy leader in a faith community is to ask questions and listen to stories. What churches place on transition profiles and websites is often less about their *actual* values and more about what they aspire to be. What was I searching for were clues about the congregation's actual values. Tod Bolsinger writes in *Canoeing the Mountains* that "culture is the combination of *actual* values and concrete actions that shape the warp and woof of organizational life" (73). Culture is found in the stories a community holds as important, sort of an unofficial canon. Who are the community's heroes? What about their proud moments? When were they most like a community? What were some challenging moments and how did they navigate those difficulties? Who are the pariahs of the community?

After extending a few invitations for coffee and convening a few story-sharing exercises with a particular parish as a whole, I was able to piece together a bit of the actual story of the congregation. What emerged from the stories was a deep undercurrent of faithfulness, generosity, and hospitality as well as a difficult past with money. There was an affinity for a few parishioners of blessed memory who had extended a gracious welcome to many who currently call themselves members, an act of grace that was greatly appreciated. There were also

stories that the community told with shame, stories about how perceived financial mismanagement in the past caused ongoing division
in the community. Some of these stories were shared in the presence
of newcomers who, though they might have been attending for up to
a year, had never heard these stories or these names. They had felt the
welcome and generosity and they'd also heard the grumbling about
money, but no one had given them a broader context within which to
situate these stories. Sharing these stories was key to helping the congregation invite other people into their common work.

When we proclaim and respond to the Word of God, we are carrying and passing down the stories that grant our communities their ultimate identities. No faith community, regardless of the denomination,
exists as an isolated ecosystem unto itself. Each community gathered
in the name of Jesus Christ exists in the context of a salvation history
that is still unfolding toward God's future. When our stories and experiences become part of that story, they jump into the strong current
of people like Abraham and Sarah, Ruth and Naomi, David, Esther,
Jeremiah and Isaiah, Mary and Mary Magdalene, Peter and Paul. The
stories we share in the context of our common worship not only connect us to these heroes of faith, they remind us of our literary and spiritual connection to God's faithful people across time and space—folks
in slavery in Egypt and in Louisiana, people marched in chains along
trails of tears in Babylon and Arkansas, displaced people searching for
home in the Middle East and at the United States/Mexico border. If
we pay attention to the voices of scripture, they draw our attention to
the hurting and hopeless in our own time. Proclaiming and responding to the Word of God is not a matter of intellectual ascent to the
truths of scripture alone. It is a vulnerable turning toward the brokenness in our own time, and holding up the reality that our apathy and
disengagement from the brokenness often only makes it worse.

One of my favorite movies as a child was Dreamworks' *The Prince
of Egypt*. Even though a bit of creative license was taken with the
retelling of this story, I believe it is unmatched in its ability to convey the spirit of this epic tale in an animated, musical medium. When
I watched this movie as a child, what struck me most was the power

with which God responded to Egyptian stubbornness. By the time "The Plagues" come on, God was in full smackdown mode. Lyrics like "I bring the scourge / I bring the sword / thus saith the Lord" conveyed a power that sent my childhood mind wandering. Even at a young age, I knew that God didn't tolerate oppression. I also knew the Exodus story was canon-within-the-canon for a great many Christians.

If this story is canon-within-the-canon for many Christians, what are we to do with mass incarceration, ICE raids that terrorize migrant families, and an exploitative economic system that pushes many people to the brink of anxiety and despair? How might scripture help us to see our own selves more clearly and truthfully? How we hear scripture when it is proclaimed can radically alter what we hear. If I hear scripture as a conversation between God and someone else that I am allowed to overhear, I can easily point my finger and absolve myself of any responsibility to change whatsoever. However, if I hear scripture as pointed at me, I am likely to be challenged by what it says.

The words of scripture cease to be the "words of eternal life" when they are not alive, when we do not engage them on multiple levels. They cease to have any power at all if they only speak about what God *did* and never help us see what God *is doing*. The entire enterprise of proclaiming and responding to the Word of God is futile if the words we are proclaiming have everything to do with everyone else but ourselves. I have begun asking questions I find helpful when I am writing a sermon: *When is the last time scripture challenged me? How does this invite me to change or amend my own life?* The Word of God must break open new worlds for us or else it is not the word of our new-making God.

The ubiquitous nature of the Bible in our culture means it is easy to overlook it or treat it casually, but for the faithful, it is anything but. These are the "words of eternal life" that tell us who we are in Christ. They remind us, when we are too assured in our privilege, that our ancestor "was a wandering Aramean." They teach us that radical, sacrificial love of self, one another, neighbor, and community are all a part of the community of Jesus and when Jesus tells us to forgive, he means it. They call us away from the temptations to define ourselves by social status, power, and prestige, and point us to our ultimate identity and destiny in Jesus Christ. Gathering to proclaim these stories matters. Specifically speaking, when the Book of Common Prayer speaks about "Proclaim and Respond to the Word of God," it appears to be speaking specifically about the back and forth that exists throughout the reading of the lessons and the delivery of the sermon. The way the congregation, the lectors, the deacon (or priest), and preacher interact is pretty well scripted. However, regardless of our roles, each of us shares in the proclamation of these stories. These stories belong to the Church. Depending on the community, a certain person or group of people might be designated to *read* them, but the proclamation belongs to the community at-large. Simply by gathering, we proclaim their power and their importance to our lives. In the words of Walter Brueggemann, our gathering continues the "appropriation" of God's salvation work (*Biblical Evangelism*, 30). We also proclaim their power by sitting and listening, allowing the words to enter us, inspire our imaginations, call us to reflection, and compel us to action.

How then do we respond? I think our responses to scripture are as varied and valid as the human emotions. Sometimes my response to the Word of God is one of awe and wonder, like when I read the story of Moses who heard the voice of God in a bush that burned but was not consumed or when Jesus passes through the walls of the Upper Room to offer peace to his disciples who were stuck in anxiety and fear. Other times, my response is anger and fear, like when I hear faithful people record God as sanctioning the genocide of the Amalekites or when Paul seems to uphold some pretty problematic household codes in some of his epistles (problematic in our twenty-first-century context). Still other times my response is thanksgiving and gratitude, like when I heard the words of scriptures inviting me to walk beside green pastures and still waters or when I heard of the wideness of God's love in Paul's letter to the Romans. Hope. Empowerment. Sadness. Grief. Love. Humans beings are complicated: why should our responses to scripture be anything but?

Practically, we respond by affirming these scriptures as "the word/ Gospel of the Lord" and thereby affirm that these stories—even if they elicit sadness, grief, or pain—somehow have value for our communities' understanding of itself and with God. Once, while shaking hands after a service, someone asked me, "How can we say 'the Word of the Lord' after reading about King David abusing his power to assault Bathsheba. How is that God's Word?"

"What did you hear in it?" I responded.

"Well, I heard that people in power shouldn't do that, no matter how religious or morally superior they claim to be."

"The word of the Lord," I said. "Thanks be to God."

Even the most difficult stories can guide us to hear the voice of God. It might be helpful to think of it as practice for listening to how God might be at work in the life of someone who has a difficult story of their own.

I did a brief internship with an HIV/AIDS organization in Atlanta, Georgia, as part of a class on pastoral care. The purpose of the course was to teach students how to engage pastorally across difficult situations. As part of my internship, I was paired with a transgender woman who shared an all-too-familiar story. She was kicked out of her home by her religious parents after she came out as trans in high school. In order to make ends meet and provide for herself, she got involved in sex work despite the dangers it posed to her. She continued down that path for a while, contracting HIV along the way. After a few years, she connected with a local church that was working to provide support to sex workers. They were able to help her find a more stable job and housing and her connection to the HIV/AIDS organization with which I was interning was helping her take care of her medical needs. Her story was overwhelming and forced me to work through my own internalized homophobia and transphobia. Society had told me stories about her and I struggled in those initial meetings to let her speak for herself. One time, toward the end of our time together, she said, "The Bible says somewhere that God created eunuchs for the glory of God. I'm God's glory, honey." In that moment, without any formal theological formation, she was engaging in a hermeneutic of hope. She was another sign that marginalized people, even those of us whose marginalization has come at the hands of Christians, can still find hope, value, and courage in Christian scripture.

It is too easy to turn away from stories we don't want to hear—stories of trauma, pain, anguish, and grief. It is so easy simply to explain them away and pretend they don't exist, or to apply a religious patina to them that erases the depth of human suffering that is all around us. But pain and suffering are a part of the human experience. The temptation to seek revenge, to dominate, to control, and to harm lives in each one of us. When we encounter passages in the Bible that point to these harder parts of the human experience, we should not turn away. We should lean in. We should engage curiosity and compassion, asking questions of the stories, their writers and communities, all the while holding the reality that these emotions live within us as well. Henri Nouwen says in *The Wounded Healer*, "For a compassionate person, nothing human is alien: no joy and no sorrow, no way of living and no way of dying" (45). Perhaps we turn away from the hard, violent, angry parts of scripture because of a shame within ourselves that these emotions live too close for comfort. Scripture holds them up for us, inviting us to respond to them with honesty and openness.

We are also invited to respond to scripture through more ritualized and formal avenues. In some gatherings, a community might recite a creed, offering their stories alongside the story of the Church in a song of praise to the God who is not only three-in-one, but whose cross shows us the extent to which God will go to demonstrate divine love. Other gatherings might include a baptism, a sacrament that is quite literally an offering of ourselves to a God who has remarkably already said "yes" to us. People choose to get married after a sermon, or begin a process for formation for baptism, or offer themselves to a life of service to God and God's church through Holy Orders. All of these responses and more are responses to hearing the Word of God proclaimed. Whether we are baptizing, reciting a creed, offering ourselves to another in love and affection, or ordaining and consecrating new clergy leaders for the church, it is about offering "ourselves, our souls, and bodies" to God (BCP, 336). Ultimately, responding to the Word of God is about giving ourselves away in love to the One who loves us so much that he gives himself to us again.

The Day of Pentecost is the day the Church commemorates the descent of the Holy Spirit while the disciple community was assembled and pondering the ongoing implications of living a life *in the Spirit*. The central event of the day was the extemporaneous translation of the gospel—largely spoken by Aramaic and Greek-speaking Jews—into the languages of the known world as a result of the presence of the Holy Spirit. The result is a holy disruption and a scandalous spectacle that prompts the surrounding community to think that the community of Jesus followers are drunk. Peter stands up to refute this slur before offering a sermon. He preaches about God's work in the world coming to fullness in Jesus Christ with the Holy Spirit being the extroverted sign of the arrival of this new age. "This isn't brand new! This is stuff the Prophet Joel wrote about!"

The part of the story that is never read on the Day of Pentecost and seldom heard elsewhere is the response of the wider audience. "What must we do?" they ask. Peter responds, "Repent, and be baptized every one of you in the name of Jesus Christ so that your sins may be forgiven; and you will receive the gift of the Holy Spirit. For the promise is for you, for your children, and for all who are far away, everyone whom the Lord our God calls to him" (Acts 2:38–39). Peter tells them that their response to the gospel is to be nothing less than an offering of themselves to God.

My commitment to God happened after a sermon. I'm not sure what the minister was preaching about that day, but I remember that when he stood up and extended the call to Christian discipleship, my mother motioned for the usher to come over. After she whispered something in his ear, he grabbed my hand and took me down to the front of the church. I remember crying for half of the journey, unsure of what was happening, but by the time I got to the front, all I can say is that I had experienced peace beyond anything my eight-year-old mind could fathom. When the minister asked if I wanted to be saved, I said "yes," even though I wasn't quite sure what that meant. I went to a few classes and was baptized a few weeks later, a scene so vivid I can still remember the hymn that was being sung as I went under the water as well as the outfit I had on after I changed out of my wet, white robe. Whatever other commitments I have made and have yet to make to God, they all stem from that moment that I said "yes" after hearing the Word of God. Episcopalians don't have an "altar call" in the same way our Baptist siblings do, and the ultimate offering of ourselves happens with the gifts when we celebrate the Eucharist, but in a sense, what we do right after we hear the Word of God is an oblation. When we hear heartbreaking stories of longing and exile and we respond with tears or sorrow, I believe that is an offering that is pleasing to God. The same is true when we respond with wonder to stories of God's mighty acts or conviction when we hear stories where injustice is dismantled. Whether we do so formally or not, responding to the proclamation of the word of God is an act of self-offering.

There is also a bit of wordplay that I've picked up on that may or may not be intentional. It has to do with what we mean when we say "Word of God." Do we mean Jesus? Do we mean the Holy Bible? The answer is "yes." In *Being Christian*, Rowan Williams says that "Christians are people who expect to be spoken to by God. . . . The baptized Christian is someone who is in the habit not just of speaking to God, but listening—indeed, listening *so as* to be able to speak. The Christian listens for God and listens in the company of other believers to those texts that, from the very beginnings of the Christian community, have been identified as carrying the voice of God" (21–22). The thought that we gather in community to actually *hear from God* is challenging to say the least. It's a disrupting question. *What if we actually believed we'd meet God in worship?* What if, instead of settling for talk *about* God, we dared to believe that we actually get to talk *to* God and that this God *talk back?* How might this deepen our own discipleship journeys if God was not seen as some transcendent being that had to be dragged into our presence kicking and screaming, but a God who wants to be known, indeed *is* known? Part of what we mean when say "Word of God" is that what we are hearing not only tells us something about God but actually helps us to hear the voice of God. The catechism says that the Bible is "the Word of God because God inspired human authors and because God still speaks to us through the Bible" (BCP, 853).

When we say "Word of God," we also mean Jesus Christ. This way of hearing the phrase "Word of God" calls our attention to the poetic prologue to the Gospel of John:

> In the beginning was the Word, and the Word was with God, and the Word was God. He was in the beginning with God. All things came into being through him, and without him not one thing came into being. What has come into being in him was life, and the life was the light of all people. The light shines in the darkness, and the darkness did not overcome it. . . . And the Word became flesh and lived among us, and we have seen his glory, the glory as of a father's only son, full of grace and truth. (John 1:1–5, 14)

In case we are tempted to assume that Jesus as the Word of God is some ethereal, theological concept, it might be helpful to hear the voices of those for whom Jesus as the Word of God is an impactful, liberating encounter. During the transatlantic slave trade, white European and American slave owners used the written Word of God as a tool to dehumanize and dominate African people. They would isolate portions of scripture that affirmed slavery while ignoring the broader context of liberation. In some parts of the Americas, huge portions of the Bible were removed to keep this message of liberation from getting out, possibly inspiring slave revolts or other forms of resistance. In this context, Jesus as the Word of God was shown to be powerful. Responding to a white missionary, a freedwoman in South Carolina said, "Oh! I don't know nothing! I can't read a word. But oh! I read Jesus in my heart, just as you read him in the book . . . I read and read him here in my heart just as you read him in the Bible, O . . . my God! I got him! I hold him here all the time. He stay with me!" (Albert J. Raboteau, *Slave Religion*, 242).

For Christians, the Words of God—scripture and logos— collide in the moment of proclamation and when we say "Proclaim and Respond to the Word of God," we mean both. We are responding to the words found in scripture, words written by imperfect human hands expressing imperfect human emotions and experiences about their journey to find and be found by a perfect God. We are also responding to the Word from whom and through whom all things were made, in whom "we live and move and have our being" (Acts 17:28). We are responding to God's own love, which draws us to God like river being drawn into the ocean.

If my relationship status with the Bible used to be "it's complicated," little has changed. It's the complex work of complex people inspired by the Spirit. That we have it at all is a miracle. It does, however, give me a lot to respond to, especially when I think about it inviting me to walk with God through the Red Sea, across the Jordan, along green pastures and still waters, by the rivers of Babylon, by the Sea of Galilee, by the empty tomb, to the uttermost parts of the world. Toward the end of *Inspired*, Rachel Held Evans writes:

> If the biggest story we can imagine is about God's loving and redemptive work in the world, then our lives will be shaped by that epic. If the biggest story we can imagine is something else, like religious nationalism, or "follow your bliss," or "he who dies with the most toys wins," then our lives will be shaped by those instead. (218)

I, for one, want my life shaped by the former. Even if it's complicated, it's life-giving for sure.

CHAPTER SIX

Pray for the World and the Church

Rejoice always, pray without ceasing, give thanks in all circumstances; for this is the will of God in Christ Jesus for you.

(I Thess. 5:16–18)

I AM NOT SURE WHAT MY FIRST WORDS WERE, but I'd like to think they were some form of prayer, even if that is a categorical nonfiction. The first prayer I learned as a child was,

> Now I lay me down to sleep,
> I pray the Lord my soul to keep.
> If I should die before I wake,
> I pray the Lord my soul to take.

In retrospect, that prayer was both utterly terrifying and wonderfully Christian. Inviting children to daily contemplate the reality of their own mortality is a bold move. More deeply than that, however, I learned early in life that prayer was a way of communicating with God, a God who loved me and was incredibly interested in even the most mundane events of my life. At one point in my childhood, I found myself literally talking to God as if I were talking to a good friend, recounting how I really wanted Bethany's Polly Pocket or how much I enjoyed the sweet taste of the honeysuckle that grew on the fence on the far end of my elementary school playground. Adult skepticism and cynicism had yet to creep in and at that age, I knew unequivocally that God was real.

Children tend to learn their earliest values from the adults around them during those formative years. If a parent or guardian demonstrates prayer at home and lives in such a way that a connection to God is seen as important, prayer is likely to be something a child comes to

65

see as important. If a parent or guardian does not pray in ways that are visible to children, it is likely that the child will see prayer or connection to God as something with little or no value. Though it is often a losing conversation in many program-addicted faith communities, the best faith formation for children and youth comes from parents or guardians who are committed to demonstrating the importance of their faith at home. The best way to raise children who take their faith seriously is for parents and guardians to take their faith seriously. This has implications for the ways that faith communities think about how to support the Christian discipleship of parents, other guardians, and other adults with proximity to young children.

I learned to pray from the adults in my life who claimed a connection to God. I remember many Saturday mornings where my mother, unaware of the *ora et labora* tradition of Benedictine spirituality, would turn on a gospel record and vacuum while singing BeBe Winans' "In Harm's Way." My grandmother did the same thing, though her music was a little older. I still hear her humming a hymn whenever I wash dishes. Gardening, running errands, even getting the mail from the mailbox were frequently found in the context of prayer and worship. To this day, Sunday morning is incomplete without the latest gospel music coming across the airwaves from the local hip hop and R&B station that decided to get religion between the hours of 6 a.m. and 12 noon on Sunday mornings. From these examples, I learned that prayer wasn't just something we did at the *end* of the day—prayer was something we did all the time.

The way my church thought about prayer was likewise deep and abiding. Each Saturday morning, my mother would take me to the 8:00 a.m. intercessory prayer service. This service was an hour of extemporaneous prayer by whoever felt led by the Spirit. Some Saturdays the service was filled with silence and a few interruptions of quiet mumbling and whispered prayers, like those of Hannah, praying earnestly and silently for God's blessing. Other Saturdays it was a loud, charismatic experience where some of the intercessors would speak in tongues. Others would try, often with hilarious results. Regardless, the gathered community would pray for the church, the pastor, the community, the world, the sick, and the dying. While the first prayer I learned was concerned only about my well-being and that of my soul, intercessory prayer taught me that prayer was for other people as well. I could use my communication with God to extend care and compassion for other people—even those I had never met. I could do more than invite God into the mundane details of my life: I could intercede on behalf of others who needed my prayers. In this way, prayer opened me up to the world in new ways.

A few years ago, when I was having trouble with my prayer life, a spiritual director pointed out something I had never thought about.

"Tell me about your prayer life," he asked. It's an incisive question I had learned to ask people who come to me seeking spiritual guidance.

"Well," I said, "I say the Office, and I stop throughout the day to give thanks to God."

The spiritual director folded his hands in his lap. "That sounds like a lot of speaking. When are you quiet?"

"Excuse me?" I said.

"Prayer is not one-way communication. As with any relationship, it is two-way communication. Maybe your struggle with prayer is rooted in the reality that you've been exerting so much effort but not resting in the words God wants to return to you. Try listening."

This counsel was hard for me. In many ways, I like to think of myself as a person with an active interior life. I am what some people would call a "ponderer." I am the person in meetings who seldom says something, but when I do, it will be something I've been thinking about for a while. What I have learned is that even this interior pondering is still noise. When I fill my mind with what I think or what I want to say or the things that bother me, I allow that noise to crowd out the voice of God, the voice that often wants to remind me that I am beloved. To be clear, our concerns matter deeply to God, but in order to hear from God, we have to actively cultivate the space necessary to actually listen. Like Elijah in the cave, it is easy to assume that God's voice is in the noise of the storm, the fire, or the earthquake. Our world would have us believe this. It is the noisy, the loud, the bombastic that our society rewards with attention. But if Elijah's witness is anything at all, it suggests that God might best be found in smallness, stillness, and peace. It is hard to find that calm, particularly in moments when our own lives are so filled with chaos, but seeking peace is not merely a matter of indulgence, it is a matter of survival. Following this counsel, I slowly began building silence into my prayers, beginning with a few minutes while reciting the Daily Office, or sitting silently and breathing deeply throughout the day. As the intervals of silence lengthened, I began to focus on specific words to keep my mind from wandering, words like grace, hope, love, thirst, light, and give. I can't claim to have heard an earth-shattering voice during this silence, but I can attest to hearing what can only be described as whispers of grace. Sometimes I would hear nothing at all, just the space that exists when two lovers are in one another's presence, the silence of the embrace of a beloved. In this way, prayer has deepened my relationship with God.

Our public worship of God, whether Morning Prayer or Holy Eucharist or some other form of worship, is fundamentally a public service of Christian prayer. What we are doing in that moment is connecting to God and participating in God's own transformation of the world. All prayer is primarily God's activity because God initiates the prayer by calling the community to worship. The chapel where my seminary community prayed had a bell that would be rung five minutes before any service began. It was loud enough to be heard throughout most of the seminary building. This bell wasn't simply alerting people of the impending worship service, it was a *call to prayer*, and indication that upon hearing that bell and beginning the journey to the chapel, the prayer had already begun.

A few years ago, after a rise in Islamaphobic rhetoric in our local community, I took a group of confirmands to a local Islamic Center to learn more about Islam. The tour was led by a female leader in the community, a woman who held a PhD. She taught us a lot about the Islamic faith: how it developed and what its main principles are, and how contemporary Muslims live out their faith. What we heard throughout the visit were the similarities between Christianity and Islam, emphasis on prayer and good works, the struggle to make faith relevant to a younger generation, and the desire to have their worship space be used as a ministry tool for the local community. I was really struck by how she spoke of the call to prayer. "The Muezzin invites us to prayer with beautiful words that remind us of Allah's love for us." She's not wrong. The *Adhan* is one of the most beautiful prayers I have ever heard in any tradition. Phrases like "hurry to prayer" and "hurry to salvation" speak to the incredible urgency prayer deserves. This is no casual thing they are doing. In the very words of the *Adhan*, prayer is "the greatest of deeds." It is the deed from which all other deeds spring, the deed that makes all other deeds possible.

That visit reshaped how I hear church bells. They aren't merely alarm clocks. They are invitations to relationship and depth. They are calls to walk closely with the God who created the universe, who cares about the mundane details of our lives, who loves the stranger and the outcast and who calls us to do the same. When I hear church bells ring, I am reminded of another world, a better world—the reign of Christ—into which I am invited to journey with the gathered community of disciples. I am reminded that prayer is the "greatest of deeds," the deed from which every other Christian deed flows, the deed that makes my walk with Christ possible. Even if the bell that I hear in any particular moment is from some far-off tower and even if I have no intention to go to public prayer that day, the ringing of bells reminds me that God is calling me—that God will keep calling me—to walk more closely with God.

Everything the community does after they have been called together is a response to God. This sheds new light on what the writer of 1 Thessalonians (often attributed to Paul) means when they write that we are to "pray without ceasing" (1 Thess. 5:17). This is not an invitation to take ourselves out of the world, but an invitation to live differently in it. Christians are those who not only expect to hear from God, but those who anxiously await the coming of Jesus Christ. To pray without ceasing is simply to live our lives empowered by the urgency. It is to live in such a way that we are aware of all these ways God is constantly inviting us to follow more closely. Whether we hear church bells ringing or not, God's invitation to deeper discipleship is constantly coming to us during ballet recitals, work meetings, happy hour, an early morning yoga class, or in the cereal aisle of the grocery. Whether we are by ourselves or surrounded by a group of friends, God is calling to us right now, "follow me." In a sense, if lived with intentionality, all our lives can be lived prayerfully in response to God's generous invitation. I learned about this level of intentionality when I visited Holy Cross Monastery in West Park, New York, a few years ago for a spiritual retreat. By the time I arrived, my spiritual life was on a pretty low ebb. I had been in parish ministry for a little over three years and was completely taken aback by how taxing it all was. It isn't the dramatic parts of ministry that are the most taxing, it's the grating reality of the little things. It's the meetings that take more and more time away from the study of scripture, the programs and event planning that siphons away space for intentional prayer, the sheer dailyness that, until I addressed them, threatened to wear me down to a stump. This experience taught me that seminary can teach us a lot about navigating the sea of ministry, but only prayer will keep us from capsizing.

By the time I arrived at Holy Cross Monastery, my faith was hanging on by the thinnest of threads. There was a specific retreat that I went to attend, but mostly, I just needed to be immersed in an ethos of intentional prayer, an environment that is unfortunately nearly impossible in many faith communities. The daily crush of meetings, projects, planning, and supervising other employees left very little time for meaningful prayer. Most days, all I could get out was "God, help me."

Seriously. Help me.

Being at Holy Cross Monastery reminded me of the sanctifying pattern of prayer I had experienced in seminary—Morning Prayer, Eucharist, Evening Prayer, and Compline. To the average person, this list of daily prayers likely seems ambitious. I can assure you as a "professionally religious person," it is. But there is also something life-giving about giving that much of your time back to God from whom your life is a gift anyway. It's a recognition of God as the source of our lives. Time is the greatest resource we have. Money can be earned, relationships can be restored, but time is something that is wholly beyond our power to either tame or control. Psalm 144—like many of the psalms—conveys a humility in the face of the passage of time:

> We are like a puff of wind; *
>
> our days are like a passing shadow. (v. 4, BCP)

Time is the greatest offering, since it is something we cannot get back. When we give our time to God, we are merely returning to God a bit of the gift God has given to us. Making daily prayer an intention makes a claim about what is most important in our lives—not our wealth, our jobs, our involvement in the community, or even our families. Aside from the proper relationship to Christ, each of these can become idols in themselves, taking us away from, rather than pulling us toward, the love of Christ. By staking out time each day to pray, immerse ourselves in scripture, and to simply bask in God's love for us, we affirm in our lives what Paul tells the Athenians, it is in Christ that "we live and move and have our being" (Acts 17:28). It is simply not possible to live a life rooted in faith without making prayer a regular practice. The alternative is to live our lives rooted in other ways of being, being carried from anxiety, to trauma, to worry.

The Book of Common Prayer suggests that Christian prayer is "responding to God the Father through Jesus the Son by the power of the Holy Spirit." There is something rich and vibrant about the divine life of God into which prayer invites us. This is especially true when we understand where Jesus invites us to stand in prayer. As Christians, we do not pray to God as creatures pleading with our creator. Rather, in prayer, we relate to God as a child to a parent. It is important to remember that Christian prayer is "letting Jesus' prayer happen" is us (62). Think about the significance of this. When we pray for a loved one who is struggling with an illness or for migrants and refugees experiencing the fear and agony of displacement, we are connecting all who suffer to the suffering of Christ. The same is true when we offer prayers of gratitude. All our thanksgiving is offered in union with the joy and gratitude of Christ. This is a powerful statement about the meaning of prayer. Even when we offer prayers for ourselves, we are saying that there is something about our experience that connects to that of Jesus Christ.

Prayer isn't just lobbing desperate hopes into an empty void. Prayer is leaning more deeply into the mystery of Christ. Perhaps this is what he means when he says, "Come to me, all you that are weary and are carrying heavy burdens, and I will give you rest. Take my yoke upon you, and learn from me; for I am gentle and humble in heart, and you will find rest for your souls" (Matt. 11:28–29). Prayer, at its heart, is trying on the heart of Jesus Christ, to allow his compassion to become ours. When we make prayer a regular practice and when we truly allow prayer to open our eyes to the suffering and gratitude of the world around us, we can't help but be changed. Prayer helps us to stand where Jesus stands, see what Jesus sees, and feel what Jesus feels so that we might do what Jesus does—announce the kingdom, heal the sick, feed the hungry, challenge and dismantle oppression, and invite folks to follow this way of love. Prayer is not for people who don't want to be changed. Prayer is for people who realize that we must be made new in order to stand face-to-face with the horrors of our lives and this world.

It is not accidental, then, that liturgically our prayer follows the proclamation of the Word of God. Depending on the genre of scripture, we have just heard the prophets call the people of God to walk in God's ways, the complicated stories of our faithful ancestors walking (more often stumbling) with God, the poetry of God's love, the promise of a new world, or the earth-shattering ministry of Jesus. We have heard again how God wants us to live, even if we selectively choose not to listen to it.

Prayer allows us to try on what we have just heard. When we pray for the global Church, our country, the welfare of the world, the concerns of our local community, for those who suffer, and for the dead, we are attempting to see the world as Jesus sees it, a world of newness, peace, unity, compassion, healing, and connection. The point of prayer isn't to outsource the traumas of our world, but to see them through the loving eyes of Christ and then claim our work in helping to reshape this world after the dream of God.

Our engagement with prayer—public and private—can tell us a lot about the depth and capacity of our own spiritual lives. It might

be helpful to think of it like a river. A shallow prayer life results in turbulence the same way a shallow river is more visually reactive to the
stones over which it flows. A deep prayer life is smooth, unhindered
by the obstacles it faces. A spiritual life lived on the surface has little
room or patience for prayer. Prayer mainly serves as something to get
through, an obstacle standing in the way of the *real* work. A maturing
spiritual life knows that prayer makes all other things possible.

A few years ago, while serving as an associate at a large congregation, I was charged with creating an evening worship service that
would serve as an alternative to the more traditional Sunday morning service. We tried a lot of things, most of which failed. One of the
experiences the Sunday evening community valued most was how we
treated the "Prayers of the People." Taking a cue from The Cathedral
of St. John in the Wilderness's evening service "the Wilderness," we
divided our worship space into several different zones for people to
visit and offer prayers. One of those zones was always connected to the
scripture or sermon for that day. One particular week, we read about
the displacement of the Jewish people who were being carried into
exile. During the Prayers of the People, we had worshipers insert written prayers into a bowl of sand surrounded by pictures of modern-day
migrants from Syria, Latin America, and homeless LGBTQ youth in
America. The point was obvious: we have just heard about the horror
and pain of displacement in the past and now we must face it in our
own world and to ask for hearts large enough to show compassion to
those in need right around us.

During most Sundays, doing the Prayers of the People this way
took about five or ten minutes. Normally, we'd ring a bell that would
summon people back to their seats. This particular Sunday, however,
the prayers resisted our agenda. People wanted to stay at this station
and offer prayers for migrants in our own time. Some sat still staring
at the photos, others wept or read psalms. We decided to continue
the service with the other worshipers around the altar until everyone
finally joined us while we shared communion. After service, while
cleaning up, I read a few of their prayers. Even all these years later, I
still remember a few of them.

"Lord, my heart is broken."

"Why does this keep happening?

"Jesus make our world and my heart full of peace."

"God gives everyone a home. We're the ones who kick them out."

The idea that prayer is somehow a passive act is not defensible. Real prayer is an act of amazing courage not only because "whoever would approach him must believe that he exists and that he rewards those who seek him" (Heb. 11:6), but also prayer invites us to be changed. Prayer invites us to offer our hearts to God, to be taken, blessed, broken, and given back to us for the sake of the world. In response to the mass shooting that took place in a church in Sutherland Springs, Texas, Robert Wright, bishop of the Diocese of Atlanta, once wrote that "Silence is what we use to hear God speak, not a place to hide from our responsibility. Prayer is not a refuge for cowards. Prayer is where we steel ourselves to partner with God for good" (*https://www.ajc.com/news/opinion/readers-write-nov/lNh3NKdSB3Nc3cfHNwzHDI/*).

It is true that there are times when we need God to be our refuge, particularly when we are overwhelmed. One of my go-to psalms when my own heart is full of the tragedy of the world is Psalm 61:

I call upon you from the ends of the earth
with heaviness in my heart; *
set me upon the rock that is higher than I.
For you have been my refuge, *
a strong tower against the enemy. (BCP)

Fleeing to God is as old as prayer itself, but truly coming close to God presents its own set of opportunities. Prayer that only seeks to throw the problem at God while we run away and hide is not prayer that is two-sided, but one-directional and fruitless in the long term. If the Bible is any guide in this whatsoever, coming close to God might result in a limp, a changed name, a summons to set people free, a promise that requires our faith to stretch to receive it, or being overshadowed by the Holy Spirit, resulting in the birth of the Son of God. It seems that God is all for people seeking refuge, but also for people being changed to go back and face the very thing from which they are running.

That God seems to have so much confidence in us is disturbing.

Praying for the Church and the world is a primary way we proclaim our faith. By praying, we declare our belief in God and our assurance that the suffering, oppression, and pain of our present reality must eventually yield to the compassionate reign of God's future. When we pray, we make a statement that God cares about these things and that all of these things and more are connected to the suffering of Christ: the suffering of migrant children, homeless veterans, people who are rejected because of their sexuality or gender identity, and anyone suffering abuse. Prayer places a claim on our lives and the life of the world—God is real, this stuff matters, and love has the final say.

It should also be noted that one of the ways we carry the concerns of the world to God is by acknowledging the ways we share in the cause of the pain—either knowingly or unknowingly. The messiness of the human condition means that we are caught in a network of goodness and terror, capable of both incredible virtue and horrible vice. Our interconnectivity means that we share in sex trafficking in Asia, white supremacy in the United States, labor exploitation in Africa, and genocide in Europe. The clothes we wear, the food we eat, the types of activities we enjoy, and the ways we make a living all connect us to human beings we may never meet and often our comfort is derived from another's agony. Sin is so thoroughly woven into the fabric of the human experience that simply living within the current system causes another human being pain.

That's what makes confession necessary. It is important to hold this tattered tapestry before our eyes at all times while also holding up the reality of God's grace. It wasn't until I became aware of the complexity of our connection that the words of the desert Christian tradition made sense—"Go, and weep for your sins." True, there are ways we individually fall short of God's love for us each day—growing impatient with one another, failing to show charity to someone in need, assuming we don't need forgiveness, or engaging in gossip. We need forgiveness and reconciliation for these missteps as well.

But we also need to weep for the degree to which we are trapped in dehumanizing systems, ways of being from which only the love of God can set us free. Without a different, revolutionary way forward, we are trapped in relationships and systems that are centuries old—colonialism, racism, classism, and more. Each of these systems tells us who we are and how we are to engage with one another. In Christ, however, we are invited to step into God's future. Paul puts it this way, "If anyone is in Christ, there is a new creation: everything old has passed away; see, everything has become new!" (2 Cor. 5:17).

Prayer invites us to try on this "new creation" by inviting us to see the world through a new set of eyes. Where the world sees suffering and danger, God sees healing and safety. Where our relationships are characterized by brokenness and oppression, God sees reconciliation and lions and lambs lying next to one another. Where we might be tempted to see scarcity, God sees the abundance of enough. Praying for the world invites us to be witnesses of this compassionate reality, to carry these concerns to God and then to shape our lives in such a way that the world sees more clearly what God already sees.

CHAPTER SEVEN

Exchange the Peace

A week later his disciples were again in the house, and Thomas was with them. Although the doors were shut, Jesus came and stood among them and said, "Peace be with you." Then he said to Thomas, "Put your finger here and see my hands. Reach out your hand and put it in my side. Do not doubt but believe." Thomas answered him, "My Lord and my God!" Jesus said to him, "Have you believed because you have seen me? Blessed are those who have not seen and yet have come to believe."

(John 20:26–29)

I HAVE ONLY EVER ATTENDED an LGBTQ+ Pride event a few times in my life, mostly because of busyness or travel. When I have attended, I have been a bit conflicted as to what my role is as an ordained person. It's complicated. I have enjoyed the peace and community I have found within the Church, even if I can admit that we still have much work to do to fully incorporate and affirm LGBTQ+ individuals into the full life of the Church. I have been a beneficiary of the kindness and hospitality that the Church is truly capable of showing to strangers, even if the jury is still out on our "lifestyle." It is truly complicated and a quarter century into my Christian journey, I have found that it is often easier simply to allow things to be complicated and trust God for grace in the meantime.

I also know that my story is not shared by many in the LGBTQ+ community. The wounds that many have received at the hands of the Church are simply too deep or too fresh for them to ever see the Church as a reconciling, holy presence in the world. For example, I had a complicated coming out story. Once I affirmed my own sexuality, I set in motion an elaborate plan to out myself to my family. It involved years of watching episodes of Modern Family and gauging my family's response to Mitch and Cam. Once I thought it was safe, I had planned to come out to my family all at once in a conversation around a dinner table. In hindsight, I realize that I watch too much television.

What actually happened was that I wound up coming out in a series of e-mails and social media posts to which most members of my family responded by liking, sending me affirming direct messages, or calling me to affirm their support. What I discovered in that messy process was the love my family has for me and how that love only grew when I invited them into that space in my life.

The Church has not always treated people with such kindness and neither have many peoples' families. Certain interpretations of the gospel have resulted in heinous attacks on LGBTQ+ people. Whether we scale up to the systemic oppression and violence LGBTQ+ face or narrow the focus to the ways people treat members of their own families and communities as a result of how they read scripture, the truth remains that even with all the glitter and pride flags, the Church still has a lot of blood on its hands. The way forward is one of continued atonement and reparations, not done out of a spirit of compulsion, but one in which faith people through the church engage with the LGBTQ+ community through eyes of compassion, wanting to make right what was set wrong so long ago.

It's complicated.

What these experiences have highlighted for me is the degree to which we are in desperate need of peace and reconciliation. In *Constants in Context*, Stephen B. Bevans and Roger P. Schroder argue that given the increased globalization we see happening around us, we need to pay special attention to the missional need for reconciliation among us. They write, "The phenomenon of globalization, which . . . has connected the peoples in the world as never before in history . . . also threatens, perhaps as never before, to exclude whole peoples from economic and political participation and to extinguish traditional languages and cultures" (*Constants in Context*, 390). To that thought I want to add that the globalization we see happening via social media is creating the context in which we see, often through the stories of others, reflections of our own painful experience. Sometimes the depth to which our society is mired in brokenness is revealed only by looking at the level of brokenness in someone else's.

Despite our best efforts to the contrary, we seem almost locked in constant combat, fighting one another to be heard, finding it hard to display the vulnerability necessary for growth, and incapable of asking for and receiving forgiveness from and for one another. The degree to which we feel trapped highlights our need for a Savior—someone who would break the stalemate and shoulder the abuse we give one another in order to allow us to consider a new way forward.

Whether it is human sexuality, gender identity, race, class, or ethnicity, it is painfully obvious that the world is experiencing an epidemic of estrangement. The powerful and the privileged, often unaware of the effects of their power and privilege, stand on the backs of those on the margins. And because each of us is a complicated intersection of various identities, many are simultaneously oppressed and oppressor, the powerful and the powerless. Each of us has something for which we need to be forgiven and something we need to forgive. The complicated nature of our human story is such that we are constantly navigating these fluid relationships, often stumbling over one another in the process. We are a mess and the prevalence of sin only seems to make that mess, well, messier.

This is why grace is such good news, at least to me.

Our complicated matrix of identities requires us to be both powerful and humble—powerful enough to claim space and name where we experience pain, especially pain that is connected to a larger system and pattern of dehumanization. Likewise, we need to be humble enough to receive feedback and criticism when it is given to us, especially when we cause harm to another. Grace is that which helps us claim our power and that which opens us to truth when it is spoken. The both/and-ness of forgiveness is almost by design. We receive forgiveness and we are called to offer it to others, holding others accountable for the ways they have wronged us, but approaching a broken relationship with the openness and creativity required for newness to take root. Understanding the radical nature of Christian forgiveness can help shed light on the radical nature of Christian reconciliation which we enact each time we gather by God's grace as a community. We are offered the gift of forgiveness. Full stop. Any penance we do is to support the possibility or reality of the reconciled relationship, to allow the potentially reborn relationship a chance to flourish, not to force the reconciliation to happen. God's grace already beat us to the punch, and that is a cause for thanksgiving. This is a high standard of forgiveness, one that we often fall incredibly short of. The degree to which this kind of forgiveness is not possible shows us the pervasive nature of sin. The distance created between people whose relationships have been upended by trauma or abuse is often unbridgeable this side of the kingdom of God. That lingering pain is a tragedy, especially when we consider God's dream of reconciliation and the reality that this ministry has been given to God's Church.

I served as a campus ministry intern in Atlanta, Georgia, as I was finishing my final year of seminary there. My weekly duties were things like working with the chaplain to coordinate two worship services every week, communicating with other members of the community on projects, and the typical "all other duties as assigned" that come along with most any job, even ones for which one is not paid. Once, the chaplain asked me to work with another member of the community to develop a liturgy for Lent. I connected with my partner immediately and we began to work on the project. We shared all kinds of ideas with one another and began to divide up the tasks. With each passing week, however, I began to take more and more tasks from him. At that time in my life, I subscribed to the old maxim, "If you want something done right, do it yourself." Before long, the entire project had landed in my lap and although I was overwhelmed with it and my other responsibilities, I did my best to carry it, motivated by an unhelpful practice of perfectionism. A few weeks before the start of Lent, the chaplain called me into her office. She let me know—in no uncertain terms—that I had messed up. While the project I had developed looked fine, she was incredibly disturbed by the fact that I had not brought my partner along with me.

At first, I brushed her words off, dismissing them as the words of someone who wasn't smart enough to notice talent when they saw it.

Over the next few days, however, her words began to haunt me. I had made a mistake. I had allowed my own pride to prevent me from seeing the humanity and gifts of another and in the process, I had broken a relationship in our small campus ministry community. At the next Wednesday Eucharist, the words of the confession jumped out to me, especially the part where we say, "We haven't loved our neighbors as ourselves."

As soon as absolution was given and the Peace was offered, I went to the chaplain and hugged her. "Now, go make it right," she said. I made my way over to my partner and apologized. At first he rolled his eyes, and rightfully so. I deserved that and more. His anger quickly gave way to what could only be described as joy as I continued talking. I told him we'd talk afterward, but I was wrong for dismissing him and I was truly sorry for that. I asked for his forgiveness and to my surprise, he hugged me. By the time we ended our embrace, we realized everyone else in the community had already returned to their seats and were waiting on us to rejoin them.

That moment of forgiveness changed forever how I think of the Peace.

Liturgy has the ability to function on the surface for those who are uninterested in the ongoing work of conversion and sanctification. For people whose whole engagement of religion centers around the perpetuation of their particular lifestyle and worldview, liturgy can support that. But for people who want more, people who know that their lives are such that they need conversation and grace, people who know how easy it is to wander far from God when left to their own devices, liturgy has the capacity to change us and to communicate God's grace to us when transformation doesn't happen as quickly as we'd like. When we pay attention to what is being said and the actions being performed and if we are telling the truths about our lives, we are regularly confronted by the terror of our own sin and the awesomeness of God's amazing grace. The Peace lays out for us the degree to which we have been made right by God in Christ. We are standing squarely in the present with God's salvation history and God's future colliding in front of us.

This is also true for the way liturgy functions for the world more broadly. If we understand liturgy beyond the "work of the people" and more along the lines of liturgy as "public work done at private expense" and if we understand Jesus as God's ultimate liturgy in which our liturgy only participates, then the peace we proclaim in the liturgy is *not* ours alone, nor is the peace of the Christian fellowship alone. This peace that we proclaim is peace for the entire world, the peace sung by an angelic choir at the birth of Christ. This proclamation of peace is for every family, language, people, and nation. It is the ultimate, if oft-repeated declaration, that the ways we constantly hurt one another need not be the way we continue to operate in the world. Another more peaceful, more compassionate reality has been brought about by the loving self-sacrifice of Jesus Christ. A new world was inaugurated through Jesus Christ. To borrow from the Holy Myrrh Bearers, "Everything is different now." The Peace of the Lord is *with us* and also *with everyone else*.

Everything we do in worship proclaims a message of God's reconciling love for the world. The act of exchanging the "Peace" is no different. Though it can tend toward either a liturgical intermission or overly scripted, vapid exchange of niceties in many contexts, in reality it is something far more. It is a ritualization of our reconciled state with God and one another. Moreover, by receiving it from others, we are committing ourselves to sharing it with others outside of the Church community, especially since it isn't "ours" in the first place. In this way, sharing the Peace of Christ is an incredibly missional, evangelistic act. When we consider how much our world stands in desperate need of reconciliation and wholeness, the Peace takes on new meaning as we stand reconciled to God and one another in a way that transcends the limits of time and space. In liturgy, we stand imperfectly in the fullness of God's future, together with one another, with those who came before and those who will follow. As much as we would like to remain separated from people, we aren't. We are held together in the eucharistic embrace of the kingdom of God. In *Inspired*, Rachel Held Evans suggests that "the church is not a group of people who believe the same things; the church is a group of people caught up in the same story, with Jesus at the center" (157). It's complicated, but somehow we are held together by Christ. We demonstrate that by receiving the Peace of God and then sharing it with others. Depending on who you are and where you stand, that reality can either be something that is incredibly comforting and therefore something we draw closer, or something that is very off-putting and therefore something we'd rather reject.

Most days it's both.

When Jesus appears to his disciples in the weeks following his resurrection, he has a lot for which he could rightly be angry. His disciples had abandoned him in his hour of need and, even after the news of his resurrection had been spread to the community, they were still locking themselves away out of fear. One might expect the all-powerful, newly resurrected Son of God to come flying through the wall with fireballs of fury. Perhaps that's another reason why the disciples had locked themselves away, rather like the time I misbehaved in school and rather than face the disappointment of my mother, I decided to go to bed before she got home at 6 p.m.

What they got instead was peace. "Peace be with you," Jesus says. "As the Father has sent me, so I send you." This moment is perhaps one of the most tender in all of scripture. This feels like the Jesus I need most days when my own anxiety and self-doubt begin to play incredibly unhelpful tapes in my head. When I've been impatient with someone, failed to respond to an important e-mail in a timely fashion, and taken my frustration out on those closest to me, I don't need someone to tell me how much I've screwed up. I don't need someone to hold it over my head. I don't need someone to give me a forty-day improvement plan. I need someone to release the tension. I need someone to remind me of goodness. I need someone to help me see the big picture. I need someone to remind me that I am not my worst mistake on my worst day. I need someone to remind me that I am fearfully and wonderfully made even if I make mistakes.

I need peace.

I also know that I am not alone.

Churches are filled with people who know that they make terrible mistakes as parents, as spouses, as children, as family members, as members of wider communities, and as human beings on the planet. We are faced with a regular onslaught of messages telling us how terrible we are. In fact, these types of messages drive an entire industry of advertising. There are books, classes, diets, products, life-hacks, blogs, and podcasts that promise to help us suck less. The prevailing message seems to be: you are making a lot of mistakes, so here are some things to help you make less of them. What we often take away from this message is: you are making so many mistakes that it might just be that you're a bad person.

When people bring this sense of chronic unworthiness into a church setting, it's no wonder we have a hard time motivating people to participate in God's mission. Most people are doing well just to be in the room! People need reminders of the ways the Peace of God operates in their lives. They need to be reminded that each of us makes mistakes, but our mistakes do not define us. Like the disciples in that locked room, most folks need to be reminded that their mistakes don't give them permission to wallow in self-pity; rather, we are called to put off self-pity and put on holy courage. Most people need to be reminded that the One to whom they are connected in baptism and from whom they receive nourishment loves them *anyway*.

There are two blessings I have memorized for the end of the Eucharist. One talks about the shortness of life and our need to "hasten to be kind." The other is taken from Rite One. When I am flustered and the service has gone off the rails because I forgot to bid the Lord's Prayer after the Great Amen or the acolytes aren't paying any attention to what is going on, this one I can call to mind, mostly because I say it all the time to myself:

> [May] the peace of God, which passeth all understanding, keep your hearts and minds in the knowledge and love of God, and of [God's] Son Jesus Christ our Lord. . . . (BCP, 339)

Ruth Meyers says, "Whether or not worship includes an explicit confession of sin, worship is always an act of reconciliation, restoring the assembly to right relationship with God, with one another, and with all of creation" (*Worshipful Mission*, 128). Our worship is missional in that it is about reconciliation. It proclaims peace to a world in desperate need of it. Not only does it proclaim it in words, but also in action, by inviting people to share it with one another, and then inviting one another to a meal where reconciliation is always the meal *du jour*. This message often gets lost amid a cadre of other competing voices. Maybe it's our own anxiety or lack of self-worth, but worship can too often become a container wherein we thrash ourselves for our unworthiness, or even worse, the unworthiness of others. We spend precious time as a corporate body in the presence of God holding up brokenness without finding ways to hold up wholeness. If the way we worship is to proclaim peace to a world in desperate need of it, we must find ways of bringing that message to the forefront. We need to hear peace over and over again because our hearts are submerged in a narrative of conflict and alienation. We are trained to resist Good News and the way of life it requires.

This isn't new, though. It seems that God's people must always be talked into the Good News we so desperately desire. When the prophet in Isaiah 40 is writing to God's people still in exile, he is writing to people who want to hear a word of pardon on one hand but are resistant to it on the other. We hear this scripture in the context of the Advent season and the nostalgic context paints this passage with a patina that strips it of its prophetic edge. The prophet's message to the community is this: "Comfort one another, and tell God's people to get it through their heads that the time for restoration and renewal has come. The peace you have longed for is now at hand, but it will require a new way of life for you. The old ways of sin must die in order that you may live in the abundance of God's peace."

Imagine how this message would have landed on the ears of its original hearers. The generation that was taken from Jerusalem likely died in Babylonian exile. By the time Cyrus the Great decreed that the Jews could return to Jerusalem, the exile community was at least one generation removed. They had never known Jerusalem and had lived their lives in Babylon. They were enmeshed in its culture and language, and in some places, likely their religion. Isaiah's message for them to leave Babylon and return to Israel would have been a hard one. Peace was now at hand, but the community had to enact it. They had to give up their lives in Babylon and return to Jerusalem to rebuild lives they had never known. This is Good News, but it was hard news. It's the kind of Good News to which they were—and we are—resistant.

All Christian liturgy is reconciliatory in nature. Whatever we were before, we stand in the presence of God as a people "forgiven, healed, restored" (*Enriching Our Worship*, 70). Part of the work of the liturgy is to get us to a place where we believe it enough to do what it expects of us. A peace-filled people become instruments of peace in the world, truly sowing love where there is hatred, pardon where there is injury, union where there is discord, faith where there is doubt, hope where there is despair, light where there is darkness, and joy where there is sadness. In truth, it takes a lifetime to believe that God's grace has made peace possible between us and God, us and another, and us and all of creation. That news is simply that amazing.

And yet, in the meantime, we are to be people who share that peace with others, sending a ricochet of peace around the world. Our experience of peace is not a small deal. The peace we experience in our hearts has a tendency to flow outward into our relationships, working its way throughout our world. If we truly desire to be bearers of God's peace, that peace must be manifested in every aspect of our lives, from the way we treat the members of our family to the ways we treat strangers, like the person on the street asking for change and the person at the register scanning our groceries. Christian history teaches us not to despise the small things, for even a grain of mustard seed grows into the tallest of shrubs with branches so big that the birds of the air fly there to make it their home.

When we gather for worship, hear the Word of God, pray for the world, and share God's peace, we do so bearing in mind the reality that we know what many others have yet to discover—we are made new in Christ

CHAPTER EIGHT

Prepare the Table

On this mountain the Lord of hosts will make for all peoples
a feast of rich food, a feast of well-matured wines,
of rich food filled with marrow, of well-matured wines
strained clear.
And he will destroy on this mountain
the shroud that is cast over all peoples,
the sheet that is spread over all nations;
he will swallow up death forever.
Then the Lord God will wipe away the tears from all faces,
and the disgrace of his people he will take away from all
the earth,
for the Lord has spoken.

(Isa. 25:6–8)

I FIRST LEARNED HOSPITALITY at my grandmother's table. I come from a large family and before we moved across the country, we were spread out over a few towns in central New Jersey. This meant that up until a certain age, my cousins and I were raised more like siblings. It was not uncommon for us to spend the night at each others' homes or catch up with one another in the neighborhood park. I remember one time my brothers and a few of our cousins started walking from my grandmother's house and, by simply making a random set of turns, found ourselves a few towns over. As a child, it felt like a journey of 10,000 miles. I recently Googled it. We wound up only making a four-mile round trip. These fond memories were all anchored around my grandmother's table. As an object, it was rather plain and utilitarian. It had four chairs along three of the sides with one of the long sides having a bench. As an event, though, her table was a glimpse into the kingdom of God. No matter the meal, there always seemed to be enough. No matter how humble the meal itself, it was always made with love.

I grew up at her table even after our weekly visits became annual ones once we moved to North Carolina. Her table taught me hospitality through what felt at the time to be normal interactions. There were times when I would visit her while she was entertaining another family, often people I did not know. That didn't matter. There was room. Once, while in college, a few friends wanted to learn how to make authentic southern fried chicken. I invited them to visit my grandmother, who not only opened her kitchen for a bunch of amateurs to experiment with deep frying chicken, but she even stood over us, teaching us how to use paper bags to coat the chicken. To be in her kitchen, at her table, is to be a part of something bigger than yourself. It is to stand in a family, a tradition, a community.

A friend and fellow priest and I once mused about what it was like to grow up black and gay in supportive and loving households. Referencing a Nikki Giovanni poem entitled "Nikki Rosa," my friend said, "People are used to stories of black and gay tragedy, but they aren't accustomed to hear that I had a happy childhood. My parents loved me and I was loved well. Only people who love well can love others well and that might just be the problem with the world." In retrospect, perhaps the best way my grandmother's table taught me hospitality was in the way it always had room for me, even in moments when I was acting out my own lack of self-esteem, or unsure of what I believed, or in moments when I was in complete and utter despair. Her table began to teach me lessons on worthiness and vulnerability way before I even knew who Brené Brown was.

My first cure as a priest was focused on serving children, youth, young adults, and young families in a Midwest congregation. The "children" portion of my position meant that I spent a lot of time sitting "criss-cross-applesauce" on the floor, telling Godly Play stories that not only broke open the Christian faith for younger audiences, but for me as well. Once, while telling the "Good Shepherd and the World Communion" Godly Play story—a story that involves a lot of wooden sheep, a diverse cast of human beings, and a relatively large, wooden table—a child raised his hand excitedly. True to my Godly Play training, I tried to focus on the story, not giving the interruption any of my attention, but choosing instead to focus on the details of the story I was sharing. His excitement continued to build until it boiled over. "Fr. Marcus! That looks like my table at my house," he shouted. I didn't know how badly I needed that interruption.

I didn't have language for it at the time, but I left my first experience with the Holy Eucharist having been fed by something in a truly deep way. It was bread and wine, but it was so much more. The table at which I knelt invited me to reflect on what that "more" might be. It was made of a dark wood and it stood just inside the altar rail. When I first saw it, it struck me as something foreign, but familiar. I had grown up as a Baptist and the communion table was something that was wheeled in when we needed it. It was a visitor to my childhood religious experience. This one, however, had a permanence. I had never seen anything like it, but I knew that I needed it and that it was inviting me to something more.

My soul was hungry for something more than the religion I had been given up to that point, an attempt at faithful Christianity that too often meant women were seen as second-class citizens of the kingdom of God and LGBTQ+ folks weren't seen as citizens at all. In retrospect, that small wooden table we used to tell the Godly Play story of the Good Shepherd and the Holy Communion did bear a striking resemblance to my grandmother's table, to the altar table at Saint Martin's Church, and to nearly every table I have been to since. They are places where I seek Jesus, seek spiritual nourishment for the difficult journey of merely living, and seek an abundant and rich new life.

So far, our journey through the Eucharist has taken seriously the idea that what we are doing is not an escape from the world around us. If it were merely an escape, our prayers would have little value to the world and, as such, would not be a faithful participation in God's mission. In fact, that might have something to do with why so many do feel the white mainline church is becoming increasingly irrelevant in the United States. Similar churches are faring no better across much of the Western world. Too many within the Church have been allowed to believe that the primary concern of the Church is to serve as an escape from the world, an ark that carries the faithful through the turbulence of our times until we reach our final destination—the kingdom of God. I am sure that this theology was developed for good reasons, perhaps when the Church was enduring a particularly elevated moment of persecution. It might even be traced back to a sermon of St. Peter cited by St. Clement where St. Peter is said to have said, "For the whole business of the Church is like unto a great ship, bearing through a violent storm men who are of many places, and who desire to inhabit the city of the good kingdom" (Clement, *The Sacred Writings of Pseudo-Clementine Literature*, 184).

The idea of the church as boat became increasingly popular, but as Andy Doyle points out in his book *Vocātiō: Imaging a Visible Church*, "When we turn to scriptures, and especially the New Testament, the boat is a place from which people are called" (142). Whereas the concept of the church as an ark of safety may have arisen from a genuinely positive motive—to the degree that it normalizes the Church's disengagement from the world around us—it is not only a dangerous theology, but it also actively participates in our growing irrelevance. Doyle suggests that this inward focus is not an acceptable framework for the Church's engagement of God's mission going forward. He says, "The Church will have to discard its inward focus and become a guiding light in the world outside the walls of our precious buildings" (*Vocātiō*, 141). It seems to Doyle, to others, and to myself that the Church is being called in this moment to reclaim its place in God's mission of reconciliation and wholeness. Our prayers have to do more than merely allow us to escape the world. Our prayers must instead seek to participate in God's own love for the world, love that resulted in God giving God's own Son for the sake of the world. This reengagement might start by reclaiming a sense of awareness of the power of gathering people around God's table while also asking us to reflect on what we are willing to give for the sake of those around us.

Probably the most compelling story I have about the power of gathering all types of folks around God's table is actually not my own. It's Sara Miles's story captured in her 2008 book entitled *Take This Bread*. In the book, Sara traces her journey from indifference to religion through "an unexpected and terribly inconvenient Christian conversion" where she "discovered a religion rooted in the most ordinary yet subversive practice: a dinner table where everyone is welcome, where the despised and outcasts are honored" (*Take This Bread*, xiii). Her journey includes finding her way into St. Gregory of Nyssa Episcopal Church as a skeptic and eventually being charged with leading an incredibly well-utilized food pantry that continues to serve as a blessing to the community to this day. The entire endeavor changed Sara, St. Gregory of Nyssa Church, and many others. "I'd been raised to reject religion," she writes, "but I was finding that people often wanted more of it than the church was willing to give: more sacraments, more rites, more prayer and healing and blessing" (*Take This Bread*, xx). What Sara might say is that the problem many churches face isn't a lack of demand; rather, the problem is *who* is making the demand. Previously churched demographic groups seem to be turning away from the church, much to the chagrin of many mainline congregations. The populations that filled church rolls and collection plates in generations past are walking away from the church and what we're left with are often the folks who have nowhere else to turn. They don't have the privilege of social position that can masquerade as religion. They often bear the words of St. Peter who, when asked by Jesus if he'd walk away, responded, "Lord, to whom can we go? You have the words of eternal life." They're not often included when churches talk about reaching out to "young families" or "our neighborhood," especially when many mainline congregations occupy privileged corners in wealthy neighborhoods. They're often poor, or people of color, or migrants, or queer and transgender, or from outside of both our ritual and religious worlds. These are the folks that threaten to overwhelm our defenses if we are not careful. If we don't put up the right defensive structures, they will change who we are.

These are the wrong people, but the people God is calling nonetheless.

The act of setting God's table is a revolutionary act. While our ritual life tends to provide enough structure to ease us into it, what we are doing is nothing short of radical. If all prayer is a participation in God's mission and if the Eucharist is an ongoing playing-out and living-into the mystery of Christ's resurrection, then setting God's table is akin to throwing open the doors to any and all who hunger and thirst for justice, peace, joy, and righteousness. Yes, it is gathering the gifts of the community—the bread, the wine, the money—and arranging them on the altar table so that the priest can lead the community in offering them to God; but it is also throwing ourselves into that offering. It is to remember that as members of the body of Christ, we are connected to Christ's offering of himself once and for all. It is remembering that what is being offered in that moment is not merely for our own sustenance, but also for the sustenance of others. Like the story of the feeding of the multitude, we must be willing to give what we have to God in order that it might not only feed us, but feed everyone else too.

While we might like to think as much, this open invitation is not a Christian innovation. Robert Alter renders Isaiah 55 this way:

> Oh, every one who thirsts go to the water
> and who has no silver,
> buy food and eat.
> Go and buy food without silver
> And at no cost, wine and milk
> (*The Hebrew Bible: A Translation
> with Commentary,* vol. 2, "Prophets," 806)

The world imagined by the prophet is a world where God's gracious provision provides for all. This compelling vision is a far cry from our world where one's ability to live and thrive is often tied to their ability to produce in our society and be paid for that production. This structure disproportionately affects those with limited access to quality education, those with physical or mental disabilities, and places each one of us at the whim of an economic system prone to dramatic swings. It is no wonder so many Americans, including relatively wealthy ones, are so anxious and deeply afraid. We simply cannot imagine the world written in Isaiah 55. This is a world where all who hunger are fed. Period. It does not matter whether they can pay for it. It does not matter whether or not they deserve it. It doesn't really even matter whether or not they can comprehend the magnitude of what is going on. The only precondition is hunger and we all hunger for something.

I found searching for my first ordained position in the church to be challenging. In the course of the process, one parish even declined to pursue my application because they were concerned that I wouldn't "fit in" in their small town (white) context. Each time a classmate came back from a weekend trip to their home diocese with a job, I grew increasingly anxious. I discerned that I was interested in working with small, scrappy faith communities, the kind held together by duct tape, prayer, and the Holy Spirit. I knew pretty early on that my gifts were best suited with working with folks who had stretched the tradition as far as they could stretch and were deeply interested in following Jesus down a new path, carrying with them only what was absolutely necessary for God's mission.

But those positions did not exist.

I wound up accepting a call to serve a church that on paper seemed like one of last places I wanted to go. Nevertheless, they had discerned a call to participate in God's mission even though the system didn't have to. Their rector was a missional priest in his own right and wanted a partner to help give that missional edge some legs. The "problem" was that the church was wealthy and white, two things I had only recently had experience with, coming into the Episcopal Church through a middle-class, black parish on the outskirts of Atlanta. I had cut my pastoral and theological teeth at a historically black seminary where we read theologian after theologian who had more than a few cautionary tales about white racial and class privilege. I walked into my first call armed and ready for battle, ready to single-handedly dismantle the system and build the kingdom of God in the ashes.

What I discovered was a wonderful community that while being largely racially homogenous, was serious about trying to follow Jesus. As we gathered around God's table—this one made of stone and adorned with glossy, mosaic tile—my heart began to soften toward the community God had called me to serve. I was hoping to change them. I soon discovered it was they who were changing me.

One time, after one of my early, tone-deaf sermons, a parishioner asked to have lunch with me. We gathered at a local pub that specialized in Irish food and got to know one another. I discovered that we had vastly different opinions on basically everything. To this day, given the growing amount of discord and division in our society at the time, I am not sure what held us together at that table aside from the Holy Spirit and the best Reuben sandwich I had ever had in my life. At one point of the conversation, though, he said something that has stuck with me ever since, and changed the course of my ministry. "People look at people like me, people with wealth, and they assume that we have it made, and in many instances, we do. But they don't see the pain that is in our lives—the broken marriages, the trouble raising kids who aren't too entitled, and the amazing amount of anxiety that goes into trying to preserve all this. Frankly, the only reason I go to church is because I heard about Zaccheus, a rich man, who probably got his wealth by stealing from people, but whose home Jesus still visited." His honesty and vulnerability broke through my armored veneer. I heard such longing and desire in his voice. My lunch partner ended by saying, "Jesus came for Zaccheus too."

That next Sunday, where before I saw a bunch of wealthy people observing their strict adherence to a purely social religion, I now saw hungry disciples yearning to satisfy their soul's deepest hunger. I saw women who had beat breast cancer two and three times, gathered around the altar, along with men who had returned to faith after their friends died. I saw people who didn't have to be in that room, but were there, either out of the habit of Sunday observance, drawn by something within, or both. I saw people who, if I was honest, part of me didn't want to share the table with, gathered there with me in Jesus's name.

Setting God's table is a set up to be changed.

What astounds me each time I set God's table is not only how similar it is to every other table at which I have ever sat, but also how much different it is. Many spaces in our society—even spaces that claim hospitality as a value—are closed to strangers, especially if those strangers fall outside of the preferred clientele of the community. This is true for churches as well. Whenever I see "all are welcome" plastered on a church's sign or website, I think about two things. First, I think about how untrue it is. In *Radical Welcome*, Stephanie Spellers astutely points out that no matter how hospitable we claim to be, each of us has a margin, a line across which it is difficult for us to see the humanity of another (6). To say "all are welcome" might be good publicity, but it also denies this truth. Perhaps a better sign might read "learning to make room" or "teach us how to love you."

Second, I think about how "all are welcome," without clear and enforced boundaries and expectations, potentially subjects others—especially the most vulnerable—to abuse and mistreatment. I remember all the times a church told me I was welcome, only to be subjected to homophobic and racist microaggressions and open discrimination. These experiences were only exacerbated when the leaders of said communities told me that my role in these spaces was to "teach others compassion." Too often, too many communities of faith, while genuinely seeking to nurture a more diverse community, use oppressed and marginalized people as compassion surrogates. We suggest that it is the job of women to teach men to unlearn misogyny, people of color to teach white people to unlearn white supremacy, LGBTQ+ folks to teach straight and cisgender people to unlearn heteronormativity and binary conceptions of gender. To be clear, a certain amount of valuable learning happens through real-life relationships and proximity to individuals and communities most unlike us; however, when those on the margins are forced into the role of compassion surrogacy, their marginalization is only further compounded by once again having to serve those in power. The only way the lion lies down with lamb is if the lion is told that the lamb is not for dinner.

To be perfectly honest, both the generosity of God's table and the wideness of God's mercy are as challenging as they are comforting. I am always struck by the honor of inviting the faithful (or not so faithful) forward to receive the Sacrament and how small I feel in that moment. I am also acutely aware in those moments of the people who are kept away from the table, regardless of how dramatically I gesture for them to come forward. The table is indeed God's table, not mine, but it is always located in a particular space and context. It is often a table placed in a building that has limited access for those with physical disabilities. The building itself is sometimes located in a community with a documented history of racial discrimination and red-lining and ongoing issues with racism that often cloak themselves in niceness and politeness, but comes to the forefront when the community begins discussing issues like affordable housing and access to transportation and quality education. As much as we'd like to be "inclusive," we need to ask ourselves into what are we seeking to include people and what are we willing to give up to make true, transformative inclusion a reality. If all we are interested in is inclusion apart from the transformation that inclusion of other people will inevitably bring, then what we're really interested in is commodity, not community. This is indeed God's table, but as much as I would have liked to throw open the doors and invite the world to submerge themselves in God's love and feast on God's grace, there are so many barriers—physical and otherwise—that keep people away. On any given Sunday, there are so many people who are not at the table who desperately need the grace that God is offering, and they have a lot of good reasons not to show up. God's table is a constant thorn in the side of every community. Each time we think we've stretched far enough and opened ourselves wide enough, God's table reminds is that we must stretch wider still. Each time we think we've come to the end of love, God's table whispers to us, "More love."

God's table *is* different. What we see in front of us each time we gather as a community around the Risen Christ present in the assembly and in the bread and wine is the heavenly banquet around which all the nations of the world shall gather to drink deeply from God's well of grace and to share with one another the bread of angels. This is a table where every hostility is laid aside, where every broken relationship is healed, where every tear is dried and everyone is made whole. This is a table of inversion, where the powerful will have to surrender power and the powerless are invited to try some on in order to sit at this table as equals. This is the table where every victim of oppression and every perpetrator will sit across from one another, where the harm that has caused a rift in relationship has been absorbed by God in order that we might relate to one another, no longer as "victim" and "perpetrator," but as sibling, friend, and companion—literally someone with whom we share bread.

Each time we gather around God's table, we share in God's mission, because to gather around God's table takes humility, openness, and vulnerability. To gather around God's table is to surrender that which prevents community with another in order to remember and take up again the identity first laid upon us in baptism—children of God. To gather is to be reminded that ultimately it is neither our access to nor distance from power, wealth, and privilege that define us; rather, we are defined by that which connects us across our vast array of experiences and identities, namely, the grace of God. The gathering around God's table is of a fundamentally different character than any other gathering. It is a gathering of grace that reshapes every other gathering in which a member of Christ's body gathers.

This transformation does not happen alone or in a vacuum, however. The ability of God's table to reshape the world in which we live is, to a great deal, mitigated to the degree that those around it understand the magnitude of what is happening. It is no secret that many have gathered around God's table only to leave and commit truly horrific human atrocities. There are countless stories of Sunday worship services across the American South that would be followed by a lynching. These and other hard stories are examples of how easy it is to come near to God's grace and to leave unchanged.

Perhaps we need to radically redefine what it means for the Church to be the body of Christ. As Rowan Williams notes in *Holy Living: The Christian Tradition for Today*:

> The problem . . . can arise if the Church is seen as one interest group among others, bidding competitively for scarce resources, or seeking to control the self-definition of communities. The contribution of the Church must always be something on another level from that of the various bodies struggling for dominance and access; it must simply offer a radically different imaginative landscape, in

which people can discover possibilities of change—and perhaps of "conversion" in the most important sense, a "turning around" of values and priorities that grow from trust in God (73).

If all the Church is falls into the category of an extracurricular activity—something we do when we get around to it—then God's table remains nonthreatening and therefore impotent. It is only when we discover that we simply cannot live without God's grace laid out on God's table and lived out in the community that gathers around it that God's table participates in God's mission of reconciliation.

In order for God's table to be an engagement in God's mission and in order for our participation therein to proclaim the good news of God's kingdom, we must be open and vulnerable. We must be willing to lay aside our armor—literally and figuratively—in order to stand before God and one another exposed. Only then can our hearts be molded in such a way that we are shaped more and more in the image of Christ becoming, in the process, more maladjusted to the alienation, separation, and division that characterizes too many public spaces in our world. God invites us to stand close to one another again and again, believing that, over time, our proximity will wear down our rough edges, polishing and refining our dullness until God's grace reflects more perfectly from our lives.

Setting God's table is readying ourselves to be changed. We've greeted one another and God. We have heard stories of God's reconciling work and taken stock of where that grace lands in our own lives. Now, we turn our attention to making a radical proclamation: God is here and by God's grace we will reject the world's tribalism and eat with one another the kind of food that is only possible when we gather together.

CHAPTER NINE

Make Eucharist

While they were eating, he took a loaf of bread, and after blessing it he broke it, gave it to them, and said, "Take; this is my body." Then he took a cup, and after giving thanks he gave it to them, and all of them drank from it. He said to them, "This is my blood of the covenant, which is poured out for many. Truly I tell you, I will never again drink of the fruit of the vine until that day when I drink it new in the kingdom of God."

(Mark 14:22–25)

I YEARN TO BE WELCOMED BY GOD. This feeling is not new. I felt this during my years of spiritual sojourn where I refused to stay too long in one community, lest anyone actually get to know me and see through my vulnerable facade into the wounded, wandering person I was. I still feel this yearning deep within me as I continue to struggle to navigate what it means to live with all my varied identities: to be black in a society often blithely ambivalent or openly hostile to me, to be gay in a church that is still struggling to understand what that means in terms of hospitality and mission, to be a church leader in a church undergoing incredible transformation. I yearn to be welcomed by God, to know that there is a place at God's table for me, even me.

I have also come to see that almost more than yearning to be welcomed by God, I yearn to be named by God, to hear my Beloved speak to me, to remind me of who I really am against the relentless headwinds of hatred, discrimination, and misunderstanding. This yearning to be named by God is especially palpable when I am reminded of the incredible divisions in our society. I do live in this world in a particular body—one that happens to be black, with a particular sexuality, and with a particular set of experiences that shape how I make my way through the world and how the world interprets and engages my presence. I am involved in my community and I do have a particular political perspective that shapes my public discourse. This is true for each of us, and when we are aware of this and engage one another through a lens of humility and courageous curiosity, we might come to see how our diverse identities, bodies, and perspectives make for a stronger society. The problem comes when society locks us into a constant posture of conflict based on our identities, our bodies, and our perspectives. The social and political construct we know of as "race" is one such example. Developed as an ideology to support the European colonialism of countries and continents that were home to people of color, "whiteness" was, from its inception, in conflict with everyone else. Whiteness is fundamentally about power. Whiteness as an ideology gave European nations divine, social, and political sanction to conquer, eradicate, and enslave other people. The papal bull issued by Alexander VI known as *Inter Caetara* gave the church's blessing for all explorers to discover and claim all lands not dominated by Christians (read "white") in the name of Christian nations. This Papal Bull is why we still claim that Columbus "discovered" America, even though what he supposedly discovered was home to millions of people and countless cultures. Moreover, his discovery was but the first step in the systematic genocide of indigenous peoples across the Americas. The construct of race locks us in unequal and abusive relationships with one another. It is no wonder then that as we look at the society around us, we seem stuck in an endless cycle of violence and retribution. It is no wonder that we struggle to trust one another, to show up for and fight for one another's well-being. Our society is swimming deeply in names that run against the will of God for us.

When Jesus invites us to cast our cares on him, to exchange our heavy yoke for his, I often wonder if one of the invitations from Christ is to radically reimagine a world apart from race, to reclaim our identities as beloved. The radical reimagining of a world apart from race is not the same as "colorblindness." Race may be a construct, but it is a very real reality that affects everything from access to healthcare, to engagement with law enforcement, to employment. A world apart from race is a world where this intricate web of racialized engagement has been detangled and dismantled, not simply ignored or shoved aside. The same is true for sexuality, gender identity and expression, and class. We get to the world Jesus imagines by first understanding how our world is intricately woven around the inequality and oppression.

In this context, I yearn for God to name me, to remind me that though my body is black, my identity is gay, and my experiences and perspectives shape a certain worldview, I am fundamentally something else. Who I am is not dismissed or erased in God; rather, I am caught up in God. I am celebrated, made holy, and made whole in the embrace of my Beloved.

I know that I am not alone in wanting to experience this recreation and renewal. I know that we live in a society filled with people yearning to be seen, named, and celebrated. We seek it everywhere: on dating apps, on social media, in our friendships and other intimate relationships. Our churches are in the middle of communities filled with people who have been given names other than the ones God gave them. One of the ways our churches can engage God's mission of reconciliation is by nurturing communities that help people experience God's love in tangible ways. Churches can be places where people come to recover something they've lost—who they are at the core.

A primary way the Church shares in God's mission of reconciliation is by recalling the stories that matter, the stories that shape our fundamental identity. This happens, not only in word, but also in sacrament. When the Church gathers to celebrate the Eucharist, the bread and wine are made holy by God's grace through the telling and remembering of the story that forms the core of the Christian's identity—the Resurrection. This story—the unbelievable tale of women finding life in a graveyard—breaks open what is possible. If the relentless life of God can be found in death, then God can also be found between unreconciled relationships, in places of pain and anguish, and in the humble creatures of bread and wine.

Early in the life of the Church, followers of Jesus would gather in one anothers' homes, share stories, and break the bread. The book of Acts tells us clearly that after Peter's sermon on the Day of Pentecost, a mere fifty days after the resurrection of Jesus Christ, thousands of people responded by being baptized and "continuing in the apostles' teaching, *in the breaking of the bread*, and in the prayers" (Acts 2:42, emphasis mine). Breaking bread began to define what it was to be a Christian. It was such a bizarre practice that it prompted many pagans to accuse Christians of cannibalism since they claimed to eat the "body and blood" of Jesus Christ. Every community has a liturgy, even if it is informal and uncodified. The earliest gatherings were communal meals that organically gave way to stories and sacraments.

Somewhere in the Church's history, the regular breaking of the bread became more and more ritualized and increasingly centered around the ordained clergy. Eventually, many faithful Christians rarely received the Eucharist at all. The thing that made Christians *Christians*, the act and practice that reminded Christians of their fundamental identity as partakers in the ongoing life of Christ, was practiced less and less by the faithful. In its place was Christianity as a political force, wielded against the powerless and vulnerable. Christian duty became synonymous with good citizenship and the radical faith of the Son of God walking the earth as an unconventional rabbi became a system, a power, a principality.

Midway through the twentieth century, thinkers and writers in the area of Christian liturgy began looking for ways to renew the Church. Buoyed by recent discoveries in archaeology and an ongoing interest in the early church, Christian churches across multiple denominations began the process of attempting to recover the wisdom of the Apostolic Age, a church that worshiped, practiced, and bore witness to the gospel before Christianity was granted social status, wealth, power, and prestige. The practice of looking at the early church for guidance in the present was not new. The Church has often looked to the early church as a source of renewal.

The Episcopal Church took part in this liturgical renewal. The 1979 prayer book recognizes the celebration of the Holy Eucharist as "the principal act of Christian worship" on Sundays and other times the Church gathers for major occasions or feasts. That was a dramatic shift from the occasional sharing of the sacrament of Christ's body and blood—monthly or even quarterly—to a weekly practice. In his contribution to a collection of essays called *Common Prayer*, J. Neil Alexander suggests that this reflects a renewed understanding of Christian identity. As followers of Christ, we draw our identity from what "took place on the first day of the week" (*Common Prayer*, 14). We might be tempted to domesticate it, to explain it away, or to dismiss it as an "idle tale," but the world was forever changed when a group of women went to a graveyard early one Sunday morning and found abundant life where any normal, rational person would expect to find death. Nothing could ever be the same because of this. If God could raise Jesus from the dead, *what couldn't God do?*

The resurrection of Jesus Christ is the event that makes us Christian, the event that makes us *new*. It is not just any other Sunday morning. It is *the* Sunday morning, the morning from which all other mornings—literally and figuratively—derive their meaning. It marks the moment when God made all of creation new, a newness we see in the Risen Christ who is unrecognizable except in acts of love and hospitality, and a newness that is extended to every person who chooses to give their lives away into the mystery of his love. It is this Sunday morning that we come back to over and over again on the relentless journey "from the font to eternity that is punctuated by a thousand successive Sundays that carry us forward by the inexhaustible energy of the resurrection" (Alexander, *Common Prayer*, 20). We live our lives Sunday after Sunday in a way that brings us back to *the* Sunday that reshapes every other day. That is the character and rhythm of the Christian life.

When we gather as a community on Sundays, marking the importance of *the* Sunday, we do so in a particularly peculiar way. We hear scripture and we say prayers, but we also do something only the Church can do—we make Christ present. For Christians, the Resurrection is not simply a historical event locked into a mysterious closet that has been shut for almost two millennia. If the resurrection shows us anything, it shows us that God cannot be kept in a box. It is the very nature of God to break out of the containers we wish to place God in. For Christians, the resurrection is an ongoing reality, one that takes an entire lifetime (several lifetimes) to understand and live into. The ongoing nature of the resurrection gives energy to our Christian ministry as we continue to engage God's mission in our contexts. We do not talk about things we have not experienced or seen. Christ is present in our midst and, scandalously, Christ is present in humble elements of bread and wine, food and drink not only for our earthly journey, but a foretaste of the heavenly banquet. Over and over again, Christ comes among us to feed our hungry souls, souls hungry for justice in a world tangled in intersectional webs of oppression, souls hungry for peace in a world caught in a seemingly endless cycle of retribution and violence, souls hungry for renewal in a world that seems exhausted and anxious. Jesus, over and over again, pours himself out in our midst, shows up in bread and wine, and then invites us to eat, to drink, to be satisfied. And all of this happens each Sunday in any given church.

Making Eucharist is what Christians do.

God's mission is reconciliation, to "restore all people to unity" to God's self and one another in Christ, to repair what sin has broken, and to redeem what sin has taken captive. This is work that we cannot do on our own and the good news is that we don't have to. This is work that God is doing all around us at all times and is constantly inviting us to step into. Making Eucharist is a direct engagement in this mission. It is making God's grace available to the world, not just the inside crowd. It is setting the table and going out into the highways and byways, into the ghettos and barrios, under the bridges, into the suburbs and compelling all kinds of people to come in, to be filled, to be loved, and to be seen.

To be named.

The Eucharist is the ultimate act of resistance and civil disobedience. It proclaims, over and over again, not only that "Jesus is Lord," but that he is here, now, in the midst of whatever is going on around us, and he's going to keep on showing up as we journey with God into the fullness of God's reign. Making Eucharist every Sunday is the Church's proclamation that the Savior of the World has not left the world to fend for itself nor has God grown weary of our warring madness or refusal to heal and support one another. When we make Eucharist, we tell the world that God has shown up again and again to continue to draw the world back from the brink of death.

The Church makes Eucharist by asking God to be present and, during that prayer, reminding the community of all the ways God has been present in the life of the world, even if we are constantly tempted to forget it. It is a story I often forget, which is why I need Jesus, I need his Church, I need the Eucharist every week, as often as I can, to remind me of the story that matters, the story that makes me *me*, the story from which all of our own faith stories, indeed the story of the world, take new meaning.

As a child, I loved the movie *The Lion King*. My regular after-school habit was to walk home from my elementary school one town over, make myself a snack, and put our VHS copy of *The Lion King* into our VCR. I did this so often that I had the entire movie memorized. I would often recite the movie as my younger brother and I drifted off to sleep in the room we shared. My favorite part of the movie was when Rafiki went to visit Simba in the jungle. By this time in the movie, Simba, encouraged by his sinister uncle Scar, has run off, being falsely accused of causing his father's death. Simba, eager to forget his past, finds his way into the company of a community that teaches him a famous, if unhelpful, philosophy: *Hakuna Matata* or "no worries." When Rafiki finds Simba, a lot of time has passed, but Simba's attempt to forget his past has not worked. Rafiki invites Simba to follow him, suggesting that Simba's father, Mufasa, is still alive. Simba was hungry for reconciliation and, buoyed by this desire, follows Rafiki through the thick jungle until they appear at a placid body of water. Rafiki touches the tip of his staff to the water and, in the ripples, Simba sees the likeness of his father. Suddenly, storm clouds gather and the veil between time and eternity is torn in two as Mufasa steps out onto the thundering clouds to remind Simba who he is. The refrain that echoes as Mufasa retreats back into the clouds is "remember who you are. Remember who you are."

"Remember who you are" might as well play on a continuous loop as the community of Jesus recalls God's saving deeds throughout history. The 1979 prayer book contains six forms of the Eucharistic Prayer, two in Rite I or "Elizabethan" language and four in Rite II or "modern" language. I reject the use of "traditional" and "contemporary" language because one hopes that all the prayers offered in the Christian community are in continuity with the tradition of the Church handed down through the centuries and, being that all prayer happens in a context and in a particular time, all prayer is "contemporary." Each prayer attempts to recall the saving deeds of God in its own way, helping the faithful remember who God is and, in the process, who we are in light of that reality.

The typical Eucharistic Prayer in the American prayer book has roughly six parts, though there are some variations. First, the prayer begins with a bit of dialogue known as the *Sursum Corda* or "lift up your hearts." This is an invitation for the community to give thanks to God, something the whole service is doing, but the Great Thanksgiving is doing intentionally. Second, the prayer continues with a Proper Preface, which highlights the themes of the day. While the fullness of God's saving work is happening all the time, the preface highlights a particular facet of God's saving work that is especially applicable on a given day, like the invitation to repentance in Lent or the new baptismal community during Ordinary Time. The Proper Preface goes into the third part of the prayer, the *Sanctus*. This hymn recalling the divine throne room seen from Isaiah 6 connects what the community is about to do to the divine worship that is continually happening around God. This is the first indication that what we are about to do isn't just about this community alone. What the community is about to do is about eternity and every community that has ever gathered around the divine mystery of God.

After the *Sanctus*, the community recalls God's mission in the anamnesis, or remembering. In "An Order for Celebrating the Holy Eucharist," the prayer book says that following the *Sanctus*, the priest "now praises God for the salvation of the world through Jesus Christ our Lord." Different prayers go into varying levels of depth or focus, but the main idea for this part of the prayer is that God's grace has always been active in the world, drawing us back to God's self. God's grace is especially present in Jesus Christ who walked among us, especially the dark and shame-filled corners of our world, in order to see and name people society would rather ignore. The climax of the anamnesis is Jesus's own words from the Last Supper. His Words of Institution were given to his disciples as an instruction to continue this practice after he died.

Prior to the gathering of his disciples at the Last Supper, Jesus often warned his disciples that he would not always be with them. "The light is with you a little longer," he says in John 12:35. "Walk while you have the light, so that the darkness may not overtake you." Elsewhere he says, "The days will come when the bridegroom is taken away from them, and then they will fast" (Luke 5:35). Jesus knew how much his disciples relied on him to teach and guide them, but he also knew that at some point, his disciples were going to have to carry on this mission without him being present with them in the same way. The thing he gave them to remember him by was a practice, one that he repeated often throughout his ministry. To remember him, Jesus invites his followers to be fed and to feed one another. This action reminds that we are fundamentally cared for and called to care for others.

The bread and wine that God makes holy in the Communion is meant to be shared by the community that remembers Christ and his mission. In the words of Eucharistic Prayer C, this meal is not only for "solace" and "pardon" but also for "strength" and "renewal." The Eucharist is not merely about providing spiritual comfort for those who partake of it. It is about empowering the sharers to continue engaging God's mission throughout the rest of their lives.

After the anamnesis (or before in some forms), the prayer continues with the *epiclesis*, or an invocation of the Holy Spirit, to "bless and sanctify" the gifts of bread and wine *and ourselves*. Though much attention is placed in some communities within the church to the practice of eucharistic adoration, or devotion toward the bread and wine that bear the presence of Christ, the prayers offered by the community make clear that it is not just the bread and wine that bear the presence of Christ. In that moment, we are caught up in that offering; we are made holy by the Holy Spirit; we are reminded that whatever our bodies, identities, and experiences, we are also God's. Whatever patterns of violence and conflict we might be locked into in the wider society, in this moment of the kingdom of God, we are something more, we are children of God and siblings of one another. The prayer reminds us of who we really are. We are the body of Christ, "humanity at its fullest." In this moment we remember that in the words of

Rowan Williams, we are "called to see others, and especially others in profound need, from the perspective of an eternal and unflinching, unalterable love" (Williams, *Being Disciples*, 74).

The prayer ends with a doxology, the community's final praise to God, for what God has done and continues to do. The doxology is typically offered to, with, and in Christ "in whom we live and move and have our being" (Acts 17:28). Here again we are reminded that this is only possible because of Christ, that we are constantly being drawn up into the eternal and amazing love between the First and Second Persons of the Holy Trinity. Whatever else is true, we are caught in a love affair that can't help but reshape us and reshape the world itself.

The thought of the world being reshaped by the power of love is revolutionary when we consider how often the only force that seems capable of action is hate and discrimination. We live in a world where might too often makes right and where we have bought into the harmful narrative that "only the strong survive." The ministry of Jesus Christ provides a life-giving alternative to these deadly narratives. In Christ, we see the example of one who came into the world in a particular form, one who was looked down on by those in power. The Son of God walked the earth in the brown, colonized skin of a Palestinian Jew. He spent his ministry showing the kind of radical love that is capable of transformation. It is not always "kind" in the way we have come to use that word. Jesus's love is often challenging and offensive. He drew crowds and repelled them at the same time. My guess is that if Jesus walked the earth in the same way today, many people who claim to follow him, including myself, would reject him. He simply challenges everything about us.

In every encounter, though, Jesus always invited people to step out of the shadows of powerlessness or abusive power and into the reign of God that had come close to them. Some, like the disciples, like Bartimeaus, like Mary Magdalene, took him up on his offer. They stepped out of the obscurity of sin and destruction and chose to stumble down the path of love. Others, like the rich young man or like the crowd that walked away after he invited them to "eat his flesh and drink his blood," decide that the cost of discipleship is simply too much. In every instance, Jesus kept going, refusing vengeance and retribution. He simply loved people to life and those people, in turn, loved others to life, and so on and so on, until you and me. Each one of us who follows the way of Jesus does so because of an unbroken line of love that extends back to Jesus himself. It is slow and tedious, but it is the kingdom of God, which is like seeds sown, coins found, and tables set.

Being named by God is about accepting Jesus's invitation to stumble down the path of love over and over again. It involves hearing this story over and over again, choosing to believe it, and choosing to live in the world that is possible because it is true. It means being constantly reminded that not only is the kingdom of God near to us, but that is in fact within us and that we are tasked with carrying it out into the world. Being named by God is about learning to see that not only has God's Spirit made bread and wine capable of bearing the presence of God's Son, but that this same Spirit makes us capable of doing the same.

And where the Spirit of God is, there is liberty.

Making Eucharist is about Jesus showing up and us believing that the Son of God actually shows up in the scandalous humility and oddity of bread and wine. It is also about the ramifications of that divine visitation. It is also about us being named and claimed again and again. It is about us interrupting the dangerous, violent tapes of our wider world with the sweet song of God's grace. To be a follower of Jesus is to take on a new identity. We don't merely follow his teachings, we become one with him in baptism and he renews that oneness each time we share the Holy Eucharist. It is a regular reminder of who we are, fundamentally, in the middle of a world suffering from a deadly case of amnesia. In Christ, we are no longer merely creatures of God, creatures that, like all created things, are doomed to die. In Christ, we are children, daughters, and sons of God who, like Jesus the Son of God, share an intimate, loving, and dynamic relationship with God. This dynamism is not merely intended to serve ourselves. Like Christ, we are called to serve the world, crossing boundaries, blessing, serving, and giving as Jesus did.

CHAPTER TEN

Break the Bread

Just before daybreak, Paul urged all of them to take some food, saying, "Today is the fourteenth day that you have been in suspense and remaining without food, having eaten nothing. Therefore I urge you to take some food, for it will help you survive; for none of you will lose a hair from your heads." After he had said this, he took bread; and giving thanks to God in the presence of all, he broke it and began to eat. Then all of them were encouraged and took food for themselves. (We were in all two hundred and seventy-six persons in the ship.) After they had satisfied their hunger, they lightened the ship by throwing the wheat into the sea.

(Acts 27:33–38)

What does it mean to be "Christian"?

This is a live question, particularly in a deeply divided society throwing around words like "evangelical," "liberal," and "fundamentalist" as though they were verbal hand grenades. Honestly, this argument is not new. It is nearly as old as Christianity itself. Followers of Jesus have long argued about whether it is belief, or action, some combination of the two, or something else altogether that makes one a follower of Jesus. The earliest conflict, one that resulted in the Council of Jerusalem, the first Ecumenical Council of the Church, revolved around whether Christianity was a solely Jewish movement or not. One group believed that Christianity was a type of Judaism and, as such, followers of Christ had to obey Jewish customs like circumcision. The other group, headed by the Apostle Paul—the group that eventually won the debate—suggested that Christianity was something else altogether. When the first Gentile converts heard about Jesus, something changed in them. In the preaching of the apostles and the ministry and witness of the churches in their communities, they had seen something of the kingdom of God. The Spirit, it seems, is always eager to break beyond the boundaries we create.

The unpredictable nature of the Spirit is a great idea to claim until that unpredictability affects us. I am often eager to know what anchors me amid the changes and chances of this life. Like Paul in the storm, I need something meaningful that provides structure and stability when the rest of my life is completely out of control.

What it means to follow Jesus is a very important question and as a person who claims to be a disciple of Jesus Christ, I have a stake in this conversation. I know that my proximity to Christ has changed my life and I want to know how best to live out that transformation. As a person who wants to invite others into Christian discipleship, I want to know what it is that I am inviting people into and I want to know how best to help them follow the way of Jesus—a redemptive path that has transformed, and continues to transform, my life.

My work as a priest has allowed me to be involved in a few conversations with faith communities seeking to reimagine their role and purpose in the context of God's mission and a dramatically changing context. Each of these faith communities is different—rural, suburban, or urban; historically blue-collar or white-collar; choral music and pipe organ or charismatic praise music and guitars. These faith communities are also strikingly similar. In an environment where a greater number of faith communities have fewer financial resources, and yet the mission of God remains, there is great interest in discerning a new way forward. How do we become clear enough to communicate the most important aspects of our faith while being brave enough to lay aside the parts that aren't necessary?

It might sound terse, but the answer I come back to is something I said once when the director of the altar guild was anxious about setting up for a service with no volunteers. "We have bread, wine, and stories," I said. "We'll trust that the people are coming and we'll ask God for the Spirit. I think we have what we need."

Bread. Wine. Stories. Spirit. Community. What if we actually believed this was all we needed?

Whatever else we are and whatever else it means to be a Christian, we are a people who share stories, break bread, and pour wine. This might sound overly romantic, but it sounds to me like a rule of life, a way of living in the world that is simple, profound, and mysterious. It also sounds portable. I am always drawn to the stories in the Bible that talk of someone's journey with God. Whether we are talking about Abraham and Sarah's epic journey, the desert wanderings of the Hebrew people, or the return from exile, there is something about our faith that consistently speaks to the power of journey. It is not purely allegory—people did undertake geographic journeys with God—but there is something deeply personal and resonant about these stories. We are on a journey with God at so many levels and, at each of them, the journey is frustratingly vague and open-ended. There is something deep at the core of our faith that speaks to this common human experience with incredible clarity.

The practices of this journey are simple. Whenever the earliest followers of Jesus gathered, they would break the bread. This practice, one that we continue to this day, punctuated their lives with divinity. The regular, weekly community gathering would culminate with this practice, which anchored the rest of their lives in God's grace. By breaking the bread, they would not only remember the Lord's death and resurrection until his coming, they would ground their ongoing Christian practice in God's divine grace. Theirs was not a once-weekly expression of faith. Theirs was a daily, ongoing, intentional exploration of grace in their contexts. Breaking bread occurred in the context of the "apostles' teaching and fellowship" as well as "the prayers." It wasn't a moment of religious duty. It was an episode of God's grace that flowed into every other aspect of their lives. To be Christian is to be a disciple—learning from Jesus, following Jesus, and communing with Jesus.

The recovery community is a fine example of what ongoing discipleship might look like. I am not an alcoholic, but I went to more than a few Alcoholics Anonymous meetings during my yearlong internship with the Church of the Common Ground in Atlanta. I also have many close and dear friends who are in recovery and their witness and journey continues to be a blessing to me. I began attending the meetings at Church of Common Ground after I was invited by several members who were themselves in recovery. In retrospect, I believe it was an attempt at letting themselves be known by someone with whom they wanted to build a closer relationship.

The AA meetings at Common Ground were as chaotic as the broader community itself. Shortly before each meeting, some of us would squeeze into the too-small kitchen tucked in the rear of our storefront location and brew as much coffee as we could in the church's percolator. The first time I did this, I just knew that we were making way too much coffee. I was assured that we hadn't and that, in fact, we were likely to run out. "These people love their coffee."

After making as much coffee as we could, we then set out as many chairs as would fit in a circle around the large meeting room. People began arriving about ten minutes before the meeting. Church of Common Ground serves members of the community who were experiencing chronic homelessness and for whom "arriving" was often a big ordeal. They would often bring in large bags filled to the brim with what may have been their only earthly belongings and placed them behind their chairs. The slow trickle of people soon picked up and, just before the meeting began, as if summoned by some inaudible bell, the majority of the community would arrive. When 11 a.m. rolled around, the door to the meeting room was closed, and the liturgy began.

When the time came for people to share, I was given the awesome, holy privilege of hearing some amazing stories of struggle, triumph, failing, and trying again. At the end of each story, someone in the community, using a woman with a loud, raspy voice, would respond, "Thanks for sharing." This was true whether the story shared was someone recounting twenty-four months of sobriety or someone talking about having had a drink the night before. The point wasn't perfection. The point, from what I could gather, was trying, making the decision to be sober in this moment, and then the next, and then the next. At the end of the meeting, the same woman who led the community in responding to each story with "thanks for sharing" would lead the community in their familiar refrain: "Keep coming back 'cause it works if you work it but you gotta work it every day." She would always add "and night!" The community would then disperse, taking with them their possessions, a Styrofoam cup of hastily prepared coffee, and, hopefully, a renewed sense of hope and resolve to stick to the path of sobriety. The road to sobriety was paved one decision at a time.

Once, a friend in recovery shared with me that he was celebrating two years sober. I was so proud of him and talked about what an amazing achievement it was for him to have maintained sobriety. I too often tend to think of journeys like sobriety in terms of distance traveled. My friend pointed my attention to the moment, to the steps being taken in that moment to sustain his sobriety. "What's most important is the next moment," he said. "The journey is worth celebrating, but it is the ongoing decision to stay sober that matters most."

There is a lot that the Church can learn from AA meetings.

A few years ago, while preparing to baptize a father and his three children, I was asked about sin. This particular family was coming to the Christian faith from a New Age faith community and wanted to know what Christians meant when we used the word "sin." My sense was that, at some point, they had rejected the language of Christianity as harmful, choosing to walk what felt to them at the time as a more open path. As this family shared their story with me, that path kept bringing them back to Jesus Christ and so they wanted to know about baptism and sin.

As a dutiful Episcopal priest, I recited to them the definition found in the prayer book—sin as "the seeking of our own will instead of the will of God, thus distorting our relationship with God, with other people, and with all creation" (848)—before attempting to translate it for a family with little awareness of the Christian story aside from a few parts used in ways that caused harm to others. I said something about sin being the seemingly inescapable network of brokenness that each of us is born into and, unless we choose to submit our lives to God whose love both sets us free and empowers us to make different choices, this network will continue to cause harm to ourselves and one another. "We can't do it ourselves," I said. "We needed the intervention of God and we need the ongoing support of a community of wholeness to help us walk the path of the faith."

"That sounds a lot like recovery," the father said, pulling a metallic "5 Years Sober" token out of his pocket. "I had to learn to submit to a higher power and make better choices if I was going to stop hurting myself and the people I love."

After Peter the Apostle gave his rousing Pentecost sermon, the crowd that heard him felt so moved, so "cut to the heart," that they wanted to know what they must do to be saved. He invited them to be baptized and receive the Holy Spirit. Three thousand people were baptized and "they devoted themselves to the apostles' teaching and fellowship, to the breaking of bread and the prayers" (Acts 2;42). In short, Peter's invitation wasn't to a singular moment of transformation. Rather, Peter's invitation was to an encounter with Christ and an ongoing journey of recovery from the intoxicating powers of sin and death. He invited them into a way of life that was freeing, abundant, and grace-filled. They were invited to discipleship—the journey of unlearning the ways of sin and learning the ways of Jesus. Mission, renewal, the faithful ministry of the Church requires an ongoing commitment to discipleship.

In his book *Being Disciples*, Rowan Williams frames discipleship as an ongoing state of being: "What makes you a disciple is not turning up from time to time. Discipleship may literally mean 'being a student,' in the strict Greek sense of the word, but it doesn't mean turning up once a week for a course (or even a sermon). It is not an intermittent state; it's a relationship that continues" (2). Discipleship is a journey. It is an ongoing, transformational encounter with the Risen Christ across all the areas of our lives. It's not simply a relationship that can be boxed into an hour every other Sunday. To be a disciple means we have to show up, over and over again, in ways that are often uncomfortable and vulnerable, but that, over time, reveal within us something of the kingdom of God. It has to affect everything: from the way we spend our money to the way we build relationships to the way we show up in the public square for one another. Discipleship is an all-encompassing, all-inclusive journey anchored in the regular breaking of the bread, the practice of returning, with our community, to the source of all goodness.

Many Christians tend to view their faith as a weekly (biweekly, monthly, semiyearly) encounter with Christ in community. There might be some engagement with faith during the week, but very little of it is intentional. The excuse that is often given is busyness. People's lives are simply overflowing with things to do, and this includes the Christian faithful. Times for prayer, devotion, the study of scripture, and acts of service to the vulnerable are squeezed out almost entirely. To be "Christian" for many has little to do with ongoing discipleship and transformation; rather, it means claiming an association with the Christian faith generally and coming to church when you have time. The vision of a transformational journey of Christian discipleship is simply a long way off for many people who are drowning in anxiety.

I don't mention this with any harsh judgment. I am reminded here of the Apostle Paul's words to the Roman church, narrating his inner conflict. "For I do not do the good I want, but the evil I do not want is what I do" (Rom. 7:19). The desire to do better is often eclipsed by something that feels more powerful and none of us is immune to this. I am also caught up in what society expects and demands of us. Because of the pervasive nature of sin, we are caught in networks and systems that demand so much of our time that we seldom have time for leisure, rest, reflection, and faith. We are told that our value is measured by what we produce, so we spend our lives making and doing, in effect orienting our lives around a false reality. If we take a step back from the busyness of our lives, we might see how caught we are in this network and how, over time, it wrings the joy from our lives.

If we truly want to live the abundant life that Jesus wants for us, we have to admit first that we need help. Too often we are unable or unwilling to admit that our current ways of being are killing us. We have to choose to submit our lives to God and make a different set of choices. The earliest converts of the Christian faith were those who could look around and see that the hope-filled vision painted by Peter was a far cry from the current reality of their lives. They were caught in a seemingly inescapable network of brokenness from which only the Risen Christ offered an alternative. To walk the road of Jesus meant a commitment to an alternative way of life.

This same invitation is offered to us today and every day.

Discipleship is not learning random facts and figures about Jesus and the Christian faith just in case we ever find our way onto the stage of Heavenly Jeopardy. Discipleship is submitting our lives to a new way of life. It is being the clay in the hands of the potter, yielding our will to that of the potter in order that the clay that has been marred in the potter's hand might be made into something new, something beautiful, something holy. It means being present and active in the process, remaining mindful not simply of the distance traveled, but also of the step being taken in this moment.

The wisdom that has come down through the centuries of Christian practice is that this transformation happens when we intentionally adopt a new, alternative way of life—a *rule* of life. It is tempting to think of a rule of life as something that only the "professionally religious" are called to do, clergy and monastics, but this would be wrong. Breaking the bread is a practice that connects us to Christians across the centuries who have found ways of walking with Jesus in ongoing, life-giving ways. We don't break bread outside of a broader liturgical and communal context. We break bread in the context of a community within which we are held and to which we are accountable. This community also shares stories and invites us to see our stories therein. The breaking of the bread is action that grounds our life in Christ.

Adopting a rule of life is also something deeper. Fundamentally, it is an admission that we are powerless against sin and death and, if left to our own devices, we tend to wander from the grace of God. It doesn't matter how much we want to follow God if we aren't willing to make the choices necessary that enable us to follow God more nearly. The final verse of my favorite him, "Come, thou fount of every blessing" goes like this:

> O to grace how great a debtor
> daily I'm constrained to be.
> Let thy goodness, like a fetter,
> bind my wandering heart to thee.
> Prone to wander, Lord, I feel it;
> prone to leave the God I love;
> here's my heart, o take and seal it,
> seal it for thy courts above.
>
> (Robert Robinson, "Come, thou Fount of Every
> Blessing," in *African American Heritage Hymnal*)

My journey with Christ has made me keenly aware of just how prone I am to wandering far away from God's grace and misuse the freedom that has been restored to me in Christ. I am not as patient as I'd like to be and find it way too easy to return anger for anger. The prevailing culture of cynicism is alluring, especially when held up to the time-released nature of hope and love. I am too often in a rush, or too self-absorbed, to stop and pay attention to people in need. Some days, I choose not to pray, because I am tired or annoyed or impatient with God. When left to my own power, it is easy to walk away from grace.

In order to use my freedom according to the will of God, I have to give it to God. I have to anchor my life in something other than my own ego and my own desire. I have to find ways of ensuring that my life is lived in ways—large and small—that speak to the reality of God's future. I have to realize that if I am not living under the rule of Christ's love, I am likely living under the rule of sin and how often, even when I try to make all the right choices, I still wander.

Which is why I am glad grace holds on to me when I choose to let it go.

Gathering with other members of the community for the breaking of the bread is an act of radical submission to the will of God. It is literally a turning away from our own will and toward the will of God that brings us into close contact with the community of faith. It signals to myself and to others that my life has a higher authority than the anxiety, consumerism, self-centeredness, and isolation of our wider world. When I break the bread with the community of faith, I am stepping into a centuries-old pattern of subversion where my old self is slowly and steadily relinquished into God's love only to be reborn over and over again.

The breaking of the bread is a practical part of a community's worship. Since "we all share one bread and one cup," the bread must be broken so that the community can actually partake of the sacrament. Theologically, the breaking—or "fraction"—of the bread calls to mind the crucifixion of Jesus Christ, the moment when the Lord of Life was murdered on a cross as a revolutionary between two thieves, or what some versions of the story refer to as "domestic terrorists." His death is a clear sign that the way of life to which he invites the whole world to follow has a cost. To choose to live our lives against the overwhelming current of the world's death march results in conflict. To follow the way of Jesus is, ultimately, to die.

And dying is the point.

Putting "the flesh" to death is a constant theme of the Apostle Paul's pastoral letters. In Galatians, Paul compares the works of the flesh to the fruit of the Spirit. The former is "obvious" he says. They are "fornication, impurity, licentiousness, idolatry, sorcery, enmities, strife, jealousy, anger, quarrels, dissensions, factions, envy, drunkenness, carousing, and things like these" (Gal. 5:19–21). It is easy to take a list like this and make Christianity about moralism—do this, don't do that. There are some Christians who do, and I believe that is a grave error. A more helpful alternative might to be to suggest that when we live according to "the flesh"—the world that is passing away—our world is a place where these behaviors are dominant. Later, Paul writes that the fruit of the Spirit is "love, joy, peace, patience, kindness, generosity, faithfulness, gentleness, and self-control" (Gal. 5:22–23). When we live our lives according to "the spirit"—the world that is coming into being—our lives overflow with this fruit.

It is worth stopping here to explore this "flesh" versus "spirit" comparison. There is a way that some have interpreted this conversation in ways that diminish and shame our physical bodies as bad. There are whole theologies that do incredible damage to people of color, women, and LGBTQ+ folks that are rooted in the words of the Apostle Paul. The result is that people, needing the space to grow and thrive, often throw away the wisdom of Paul in the process.

I think Paul is less concerned with our physical bodies, and more concerned with the powers that are at war around us, namely the values of this world and the values of the reign of God. Galatians 5:17 says that "for what the flesh desires is opposed to the Spirit, and what the Spirit desires is opposed to the flesh; for these are opposed to each other, to prevent you from doing what you want." This again speaks to the power of sin, that even when we want to do what is right, we have to overcome incredible odds to do so. In Colossians, Paul writes, "so if you have been raised with Christ, seek the things that are above, where

Christ is, seated at the right hand of God. Set your minds on things that are above, not on things that are on earth, for you have died, and your life is hidden with Christ in God" (3:1–3). Paul clearly does not mean that we have physically died. He means that our perspective is different *in Christ*. We are no longer held in the inescapable sway of the value systems of this world. Why? Because Christ has inaugurated a new world, the kingdom of God, and he calls us into a way of life that is compassionate and just and merciful. We can live in such a way that we experience the abundant fruit of the Spirit in our lives, but that only happens when we accept that the value systems of this world are dying and choose to die to them ourselves.

This dying is a process where we try, fail, and learn, and try again. It is walking, stumbling, and getting up to walk again. It is an ongoing journey to renewal and revival. Understanding it is key to understanding and engaging God's mission. To be a Christian isn't about perfection, it is about living a life of ongoing transformation. It is about growing up "into the full stature of Christ" so that, as little Christs, we can go out into the world blessing, giving, healing, restoring, challenging, and loving just as Jesus does. Christian practice doesn't seek "holiness" or "sanctification" for its own sake. This is not about personal piety and our own salvation alone. This is about mission. This is about a movement of people who continue to have their lives shaped by the grace of God and who, in turn, engage in the transformation of the world around them.

And all of this is rooted in the breaking of the bread.

Christians are people who practice a different way of life. It is easy to reduce it to a list of dos and don'ts, but that would be too simplistic. We are a people who practice the way of Jesus. To be a Christian is to be a disciple of Christ, a follower of the Jesus of Nazareth, one who submits their life over and over again to the saving way of the Son of God. In some sense, we do walk this road alone because each of us has to choose to follow and we have to choose to follow over and over again. In another sense, we walk this road in the company of a saving community. It is simply not possible to be Christian as an individual. To be "saved" is to be saved into a community who walks with us as we all work to get free.

CHAPTER ELEVEN

Share the Gifts of God

As they came near the village to which they were going, he walked ahead as if he were going on. But they urged him strongly, saying, "Stay with us, because it is almost evening and the day is now nearly over." So he went in to stay with them. When he was at the table with them, he took bread, blessed and broke it, and gave it to them. Then their eyes were opened, and they recognized him; and he vanished from their sight. They said to each other, "Were not our hearts burning within us while he was talking to us on the road, while he was opening the scriptures to us?"

(Luke 24:28–32)

BY THE TIME WE GET TO THE PART OF OUR WORSHIP where we "share the gifts of God," we have experienced grace upon grace through the sharing of stories, the offering of prayers, and the singing of praise to God. The way we worship God says something about what we believe about God and what God is up to in the world around us. That we often conclude our worship sharing God's gifts with others makes a claim on us that is worth exploring, especially when we think about the ways our regular worship continues to revive the Church. It might be helpful to begin with a story.

Jesus teaches in a variety of ways, through prose and proverbs, but one of his primary teaching methods was parables—expansive stories that destroy both our preconceived notions of the way our world works and how we understand the grace of God. They are meant to be obscure and strange because they are attempting to convey the truths of a kingdom that is not of this world. The point of parables is not to have a point. Amy-Jill Levine echoes this spaciousness of parables when she says:

> What makes the parables mysterious, or difficult, is that they challenge us to look into the hidden aspects of our own values, our own lives. They bring to the surface unasked questions, and they reveal

121

the answers we have always known, but refuse to acknowledge. Our reaction to them should be one of resistance rather than acceptance. For our own comfort, we may want to foreclose the meaning rather than allow the parable to open into multiple interpretations. We are probably more comfortable proclaiming a creed than prompting a conversation or pursuing a call. (*Short Stories by Jesus*, 2)

Parables are amazing stories that Jesus intentionally uses to break open the mystery of the kingdom of God. When asked about eternal life, or being saved, or the limits of neighborliness, Jesus rejects straight answers. Rather, he chooses the winding, circuitous route of wonderfully enigmatic stories, stories that become for us rhetorically expansive and mysterious paths that go off in a thousand directions, double back on themselves, and yet all seem to arrive in the same location—the reign of God. They feature banquets, sheep, coins, and slaves, but my favorite one features a sower, seed, and different kinds of soil. The so-called parable of the sower (also known as the Parable of the Soils) is often used by some to shame people into being a particular kind of soil. "Jesus wants you to be the good soil," they say, "that way you will bear much fruit." This kind of interpretation is exhausting. There isn't a whole lot of good news in this kind of message in the context of people who often suffer with a chronic lack of self-esteem and worthiness. Using the parable of the sower as some kind of story of self-improvement is misguided.

To me, the parable of the sower isn't about trying to be a different kind of soil because that doesn't sound like good news. The parable of the sower speaks to me about the prodigal grace of God which God showers upon us all—good soil, bad soil, or rocky soil. God's grace is lavished prodigally throughout scripture, especially in the direction of people we would rather not see become the recipients of God's grace. God's grace visits tax collectors, lepers, women, the poor, and children. We might like to oversentimentalize this, but this is nothing short of revolutionary. At the heart of Christianity is the message that God's grace "reaches to the highest mountain and flows to the lowest valley" (Andrae Crouch, "The Blood Will Never Lose Its Power," in *African American Heritage Hymnal*). It doesn't just visit the people who look, think, and behave like us. God's grace visits the unrespectable, the backsliders, the inappreciative, and the unaware. God's grace is shared with those who live beyond our margins. This is true for us, no matter how open and welcoming we claim to be.

And God expects us to do the same.

This is what makes sharing the gifts of God such a radical act. First, we have to realize that these are not our gifts to give. This is often very difficult for the Church as an institution to realize. By God's grace, we have been invited to engage God's mission by receiving the gifts of God in order to give them away the way God does—prodigally and wantonly, throwing seed on the rocks, the road, and manure. Too often, though, the Church treats God's grace as if we own it, as if it were our personal possession, as if we were the sole decision-makers as to who is and is not worthy. When we become gatekeepers to God's grace, we miss what happens when grace is shared freely—it multiplies, exponentially, until the whole earth is filled with the grace of God.

The hard truth for us as a church seeking to engage God's mission is that God's grace is not for the worthy, whatever that even means. If it were, then we'd be a starving world with no hope of nourishment. As it stands, we are a starving world, but that is mostly because we choose not to receive and share God's grace. From an economic standpoint, we do not now, nor have we ever had, a supply problem. Scripture reminds us that God's grace is abundant and "new every morning." What we have a distribution problem. The people and communities entrusted to share God's grace often struggle to do so. This might have something to do with the fact that we struggle to receive it ourselves. It can be difficult to believe that we are loved unconditionally. We seem to prefer to talk about God's love in the collective—God loves *us* or God loves *the world*.

But God's love is as particular as it is global. It is specific. God loves me. God loves you. Yes, that is still true when held up with our personal struggles and addictions that we are too ashamed to name aloud. That is still true when we are impatient with ourselves or with others. God's love is still there when we turn away from human suffering, choosing an uncomfortable peace over a brave reconciliation.

God's love is still there when we have reached what we think is the end of our faith and refuse to take that next, vulnerable step into the unknown. God's love remains true for us regardless of the ways we deny God's goodness in ourselves, in others, and in God's creation.

I think that's why the prayer book instructs the ministers of the liturgy to receive God's gifts before we give them to someone else. Despite the fact that more and more communities invert this practice, assuming that they, not the Risen Christ, are the hosts of the Eucharist, the current rubrics of the prayer book name an uncomfortable truth: before we can truly extend God's grace to others, we have to practice receiving it first. Before we can place the broken bread in the open hands of another, we must practice receiving the gifts ourselves. Humility and a posture of receptivity must live within us before we can ever expect it from another. No matter what our role is in the community's eucharistic gathering, when it comes to sharing God's gifts, each of us is equally a guest at a table that belongs, not to the Church, but to the Lord. It is made ready for those who hunger and thirst for righteousness, for those who have no idea what they are hungry for, and for those who have become so accustomed to starvation that they are unaware of just how hungry they truly are.

About two years after I was ordained, I found myself standing behind the altar feeling truly empty. Though it was at the beginning of Advent and in the middle of a particularly busy program year, this wasn't merely a matter of fatigue. I was on the verge of unbelief, not simply doubt. Doubt is a natural part of faith. Barbara Brown Taylor says that "dark and light, faith and doubt, divine absence and presence, do not exist at opposite poles. Instead, they exist with and within each other, like distinct waves that roll out of the same ocean and roll back into it again" (*Learning to Walk in the Dark*, 96). Doubting, even walking without a sense of God's presence, is all a natural part of our journey with God. In my experience, doubt has proven to be liberating. In order to step into an abiding sense of belovedness with my queer identity, I had to doubt that the homophobic God was supreme. Doubt is simply a part of what it means to walk with God. Things regularly fall apart and things are always being made new.

What I was feeling was something else—burnout. It might shock some, but even two years into ordained ministry, I was growing to resent the work I was doing. Some of it was the sheer magnitude of what I was involved in and how little difference it seemed I was making in it. I was also tired of being on the receiving end of others' anxiety, only to stand at the altar rail and give communion to these same people. In retrospect, these ritualized moments are important. I am glad to have rituals to carry me through rough moments and strained relationships, rituals that remind me that I am called to be loving and compassionate toward all people, including people who forget that there is a human being on the other side of their anxious e-mails and phone calls. I was tired of throwing myself into work that was as thankless as it was critique-full. I was tired of praying and asking God for patience, only to find myself short of it.

In a particularly low moment, I called a friend who had been taught by the same professor of pastoral theology. My friend reminded me that this professor—Julia Gatta, affectionately and perpetually known as "Mother Julia"—warned each of us over and over about the danger of "becoming too familiar with holy things." I can remember one time sitting in her class and hearing her say, "There should always remain within us something that feels small when we stand before God." My friend reminded me of these words and, as I tossed these words around in my mind, it came to me that the crushing dailyness of priestly ministry had caused me to forget how hungry I was. I had gotten so used to pretending I was the host that I had forgotten to be a guest. I was so busy feeding others and absorbing others' anxiety, fear, and sadness that I had forgotten that my job was not simply to be a holy PEZ dispenser or an emotional sponge. My calling was to be hungry for God, publicly, to remind others how hungry they are. I was called to fall in love with God openly and, by example, invite others to do the same. The life I signed up for the moment I said "yes" to God—and the life I continue to sign up for each morning I get up and say "yes" again—is a life of feeding hungry people who often don't know they are hungry, and that includes allowing myself to be fed.

Sharing the gifts of God first requires us to recognize just how hungry we are. When I come to God's table, whether I do so as the designated leader of the community's worship or simply as a worshiper, I try to remember how hungry and thirsty I am. When Jesus tells the Samaritan woman at the well that she will never thirst again, I think what he meant is not that she would never experience the sensation of spiritual emptiness, but that she would know where to go when she felt that emptiness. Jesus tells that unnamed woman that he is the well of "living water" (John 4:10). There are many days I feel like that woman, and I can testify that the words of Jesus are true.

The fact that the body of Christ gathers every seven days to bear witness to the Resurrection of Jesus Christ assumes that we hunger, that we thirst, that we forget. That Sundays come around with shocking regularity makes clear that there is something about this pattern that is to be commended. The emptiness that we feel is only magnified by a world hell-bent on walking away from God's compassion and mercy. Simply showing up is an admission that we are hungry for something, even if we don't know what we are hungry for. The good news is that we are fed at a level so deep, it is often difficult to truly put it into words.

A church that engages God's mission and proclaims the Good News is a hungry church—we are a community that can admit, almost paradoxically, that we are never satisfied and that we are filled in ways we can't even imagine. A mission-oriented church admits that it has growth to do, that it has not yet achieved the fullness to which God continues to call it, and yet there is a perpetual hunger for God's Spirit to fill it, empower it, challenge it, support it, renew and revive it. This kind of church admits that we are often not the "good soil" that bears "good fruit" and yet rejoices that God pours God's grace on us *anyway*.

Recognizing how hungry we are builds empathy for the hunger of others. When we reflect on the ways God's grace has fed us, we can also see how much joy we are invited into simply by sharing God's gifts with others—all others. They are God's gifts that we have been trusted to share with others as God does. It's an ingenious trick to make sure we've been paying attention to everything that has gone on around us. If we are truly engaging God's mission of reconciliation, then we are engaged in the process of stretching more and more to share God's gifts with people further and further from our definition of worthy.

Once, while struggling with a pastoral relationship, I brought the issue to my therapist, a middle-aged man who identified as a lapsed Roman Catholic. In addition to helping me own my part in the pastoral breakdown, he helped me understand that so much of the other person's response might not have really been about me. My therapist also helped me understand that I could not change the other person, all I could do was be mindful of my own actions and try to respond lovingly. "But I am tired of being the adult," I said. "I am tired of being the person in the room who has to keep showing up, keep being mature, keep extending the hand. It hurts!" "Marcus," my therapist responded, "I am not terribly religious, but I think that's kind of your job."

I was taken aback and offended, but deep down I knew he was right.

"And when you are truly tired, let the ritual carry you."

The power of ritual is such that even when we don't feel like it, or can't really bring our full selves to it, it carries us into places we'd otherwise be unable to go. In the context of my fragile pastoral relationship with this parishioner, there were many times when I'd read another one of his harsh, overly critical e-mails just before worship and then, within an hour, was in the position to place a broken piece of bread in his hands. I realized that his anger was masking a deeper, unspoken pain. He was hungry, but he either didn't have the ability to name it out loud or he wasn't aware of it. Even if the extent of our pastoral relationship was that brief, intimate moment of encounter, I am thankful for that moment carrying the baggage of our relationship and continually inviting us back to the table.

Sharing God's grace is challenging, because we are often challenged to share it with people we'd rather not. One of the reasons I am grateful for the Church is because it brings me into relationships with people I would otherwise not be in relationship with. The invitation is not just to sit in the same room, though. God's invitation runs much deeper. God's invitation into the same room is to get us to the same table where we feed and serve one another. It's a subversive invitation, one that, when engaged over and over, can absolutely transform hearts and minds. This is how God's kingdom breaks in, not by war, or legislation, or by the will of the multitude, but by simple acts of love that dramatically reshape relationships.

There can be no enemies at God's table.

As challenging as it can be to truly share the gifts of God, the experience of doing so is true joy. When we realize that we are helping to satisfy someone's deepest longing in a simple act of hospitality and generosity, it becomes clearer just how the practice can inform the rest of our lives. I was always taught that "kindness costs nothing." Sharing God's gifts is similar, in many aspects. While there are moments where sharing the gifts of God will cost us something, many times the way that we are invited to share grace with another costs us nothing but attention and intention. It can be as little as offering to pray with a friend or coworker who has expressed concern about something in their life. It can be rolling down the window to speak to someone asking for money on the roadside, even if we have nothing to offer but a humanizing greeting. It can be thanking the cashier at the grocery store by name. Sharing grace doesn't have to be something big, but it can make a big difference in the lives of people who are used to being unseen and unheard.

Imagine a community of people who are so aware and so filled with God's grace that they can't help but pour it into others. Imagine people whose lives are so Jesus-shaped that they bless the world the way Jesus did. That would be ideal! That would be the kind of compassionate movement rooted in the kingdom of God that could really change the world. And because we are often not that, we need regular reminders that we've been filled, that we will be filled again, that God's grace is boundless, and that God's love is endless.

Sharing the gifts of God is a faithful practice in a world suffocating under a yoke of alienation, isolation, tribalism, and brokenness. It is good news to know that there are communities, gatherings of faithful people, who are trying, even if stumbling, to live a more compassionate, just, generous life in the world. It is also good news that the invitation to join that community is open to all who desire it. To be a Christian is simply about securing our own individual salvation, the world be damned. To follow Christ is to have been filled by God so much that you desire to fill others. And then to do it again. And again. And again.

I was invited to a parishioner's home once to meet a few of his friends. Even though they all knew that I was his priest, I tried to steer clear of that conversation for as long as I could since, in my experience, once you bring up the fact that there is a priest in the room, the conversation can be about nothing else. As we sat down to dinner, though, one of his friends said, "So, you're a priest."

"Yes, I am," I bashfully replied.

"Do you think the world needs the Church?"

Maybe it was the fact that I was shocked by the speed at which the conversation had escalated, or maybe it was the fact that dinner was running a little late and I was hungry, or maybe I was in a less-than-confident spiritual space, but I replied, "No, not really. As long as people learn to be compassionate, that's all that really matters."

I have spent the years since that conversation repenting of that answer. I absolutely think the world needs the Church, because simply learning to be compassionate isn't what Christianity is all about. Learning compassion is important and a grossly underappreciated value, but Christianity speaks a deeper, broader message, one that I believe is good news in our age. At the core of our faith we believe that God is love and that out of that love God created an abundant, rich, and full creation. Somewhere along the way, although we were invited into relationship with God, we chose to turn away, to put our individual selves and individual interests ahead of others. In the process we wounded one another, exploited creation, and disrupted our relationship with God.

But God's grace is such that we weren't left to die in the wilderness of our own making. Time and time again, God sent prophets, teachers, and sages to remind us of the road God desires for us to walk and, in God's own time, God gave the ultimate gift to us—God's self in the form of Jesus Christ. His birth, life and ministry, death, resurrection, and ascension renewed creation and made it possible to be the full human beings God created us to be in the first place. Each of us is invited into the renewal through the waters of baptism, by which we join ourselves to the death and resurrection of Jesus Christ and when we gather for Holy Eucharist, sharing and partaking of the gifts of God, we are living, in that moment, in the kingdom of God. Our deepest hunger is satisfied, the very thing we most long for is fulfilled, and we participate in the ongoing renewal of the world.

The Church, the body of Christ, has been entrusted with the sacred task of bearing witness to the kingdom of God and inviting whoever will listen to experience it in their lives. We are not a special interest group or a social club; we are active participants in the continued unfolding of God's salvation plan. And that this happens in every prayer prayed, every song sung, every story heard, every morsel of bread and sip of wine received and shared is nothing less than grace. God has put this incredible task into our hands and given us the tools to make it happen.

Sharing the gifts of God are about revival and renewal, not only of ourselves, but of all of creation. That this is the last thing we do before we leave suggests that maybe it is the first thing we do after we have been sent out. In that way, we show the world that there is still a stream in the desert and a table set in the wilderness. The Christian life is simply being fed and telling the world where true bread is to be found.

CONCLUSION

Go Forth

IF SUNDAY MORNINGS smelled like spray starch and pancakes, Sunday afternoons tasted like fried chicken, cornbread, collard greens, candied yams, and sweet tea. It felt like warm hugs, too many people at the table, and an impromptu nap. They sounded like kids playing in the yard, the soft murmur of the television in the "downstairs room," and the commotion of dishes being washed after dinner. Leaving a feast of God, we were headed to another feast, this one with a few more menu options . . . at least on the surface. The feasting did not cease when the Lord's Supper was over. Rather, the feast continued with eyes of gratitude and thanksgiving helping us to interpret the feast that was to come. The entire practice of Sunday-keeping was a rich banquet, spiritual and physical. The message was clear: what we experience in public worship is not separated from what we experience outside of it. What we experience in public worship is the *fullness* of what we experience beyond it. In it and through it the rest of our lives are held with a more grace-filled grasp and seen through eyes of compassion. The fear that stymies our service is a little less powerful, the unhealed relationships are drained of their venom, our own struggle to grow in faith is itself met with grace.

All of this happens because our gathering is not merely that of a community of people hearing stories and sharing a bizarre ritual of bread and wine. All of this happens because in that gathering, in that proclamation, and in that sharing, we have come close to God and God has come close to us. To gather as a community of Jesus followers is no small, insignificant thing. It is freighted with layers of meaning—salvation history and God's future colliding in stories, prayers, bread, and wine. We experience this depth of meaning not to hoard it to ourselves, but to share it with others, to bear witness to the reign of Christ that is crashing into our current reality. If the entirety of salvation history and God's future are contained in that moment when we gather as Christians in the name of Christ, then that must have some impact on the way we live our lives beyond the rituals and symbols of the Church. Indeed, human lives that come close to God never leave the same.

Consider for a moment, Abram. He is a complicated figure, but the Bible and tradition remember him as *the* paragon of faith. One day, as he was minding his business in Ur, he hears a word from God instructing him to get up and start walking until God says stop. All along the way, Abram—who became Abraham, his wife Sarai—who became Sarah, Hagar, and the rest of their band experienced incredible struggles as they wrestled to discern what it meant to follow God faithfully. In the end, the tradition of the three of the world's great religions—Judaism, Christianity, and Islam—hold that there was something especially exemplary about Abraham's faith.

Think about Moses. He grows up in the middle of a terrifying, anti-Hebrew crackdown in Bronze Age Egypt. Through the intricate machinations of God and a few clever women, he is not only saved from death by water, but adopted into Pharaoh's household and nursed by his own mother. After running away for standing up to the physical oppression of a Hebrew slave, he finds himself face-to-face with God in a burning bush. This book summoned him to the task of liberation—setting God's people free. Though Moses seemed to have every excuse in the book, the God in the voice of the burning bush would not let him shrink back from this task. He would spend the next forty years growing up into the full stature of the prophet and leader God saw in him all those years ago.

Ponder Mary. She appears to have been minding her own business in Palestine when an angel bursts through her expectations with a curious greeting—she has found favor with God. In her the Son of God would be born into the world and she would spend the rest of her life living out the implications of the one moment her life changed over and over again.

If our lives change the moment we come close to God, what happens when that closeness happens in the successive Sundays that stretch from "font to eternity"? The answer is clear: our lives overflow with the grace upon grace.

One of the biggest blessings of my life was the year I spent as a hospital chaplain in Atlanta, Georgia. There were many times that year when I was face-to-face with incredibly difficult moments, but every moment was filled with some sort of hidden grace. On one round through the hospice unit, I met a woman named Teresa who, by the time I met her, was looking at her last days of physical life. Most of the patients I visited on my rounds were either resistant or indifferent to my presence with them, but Teresa was excited. The first day I met her, she went on and on about her own Southern Baptist church in south Georgia, her pastor, and her community. "I've lived in one place my whole life," she said. "My roots run deep." Some days, I would visit Teresa and it would just be the two of us. Other days, her room was filled with visitors—neighbors, church members, children, and other relatives. Regardless, her room was always filled with a fresh yellow rose and a few sprigs of baby's breath, cards, and balloons.

One day, toward the very end of her life, Teresa wanted me to help her read through all of the cards that flanked her bed. One by one, I handed them to her as she read them. Each one of them shared a memory of something Teresa had done that had made a difference in someone else's life. There was the card that talked about the pie she baked for a new family in town after a young mom suffered miscarriage, or the outfits she sewed for the church choir, or the hours she had spent volunteering at a local hospital. "Everyone has all these nice things to say about you," I said. "People really love you."

"I never thought I'd make a huge difference in the world," she said, "not a girl from a small town like me. But God's grace let me make a little bit of difference where I could and that's alright with me."

"It seems to me you made a little more than a little bit of difference," I responded.

I often struggle with the idea that the lives of the saints are commemorated for us to emulate them. I get the concept, but it seems to me that it leaves so many people searching for burning bushes, disembodied hands, or an angel with a penchant for fighting. I wonder if the thing we are called to emulate in the saints isn't their actions, but their openness to God. I wonder if what we are being challenged to replicate is the degree to which their lives were filled with grace.

Perhaps the work of the Christian faithful is to spend our lives appropriating the grace of Sunday's gathering across the rest of our lives. We are overwhelmed by love each time we gather as a community and it takes time to figure out how to give that love away. Proclaiming the Good News of God in Christ by word *and* example is not merely a set of actions and practices—it is a way of being. It is regularly experiencing the grace of God in the power of community gathered, in the spaciousness of words proclaimed, in the audacity of prayers prayed, in the transformation of peace shared, in the holiness of Eucharist made, and in the generosity of gifts shared. If we pay attention to what is going on, even a simple gathering of Christians is filled with an eternity of meaning.

I have only recently found language to describe the feeling I felt when I first received the Eucharist in an Episcopal Church. I was overwhelmed because what I felt in that moment was the vastness of eternity crashing into me at once. I have spent my days since that moment trying to live out that grace, but more and more gets piled on top of it. After a few years, I discovered that I was caught in a losing battle. I tried to give grace away but found that the more I gave it, the more I got it. This must be what the psalmist means when they say that goodness and mercy shall pursue and overtake me all the days of my life.

To leave worship is not to leave the presence of God or to *begin* God's mission. To leave the public worship of the Christian community is to reenter time as one who seeks to live out the implications of all this meaning. We carry heaven into hell, eternity into time, a sense of enough into scarcity, faith into doubt, love into hatred and indifference, reconciliation into estrangement, and light into dark. We carry Sunday into the rest of the week and, in so doing, we make it holy, claim it for Christ, and participate in the ongoing unfolding of the fullness of his reign.